THE LAST YEAR
OF MALCOLM X

THE LAST YEAR
OF MALCOLM X

The Evolution of a Revolutionary

by George Breitman

PATHFINDER

New York   London   Montréal   Sydney

Copyright © 1967 by Pathfinder Press
All rights reserved
Library of Congress Catalog Card No. 67-20467
ISBN 0-87348-004-X paper; ISBN 0-87348-003-1 cloth
Manufactured in the United States of America

First edition, 1967
Tenth printing, December 1990

Quotes from *The Autobiography of Malcolm X* are copyright © 1964 by
Alex Haley and Malcolm X, copyright © 1965 by Alex Haley and Betty
Shabazz, and are reproduced by permission of Grove Press.

Cover photo and frontispiece by Eli Finer.

Pathfinder
410 West Street, New York, NY 10014, U.S.A.

Pathfinder distributors around the world:
Australia (and Asia and the Pacific):
    Pathfinder, P.O. Box 153, Glebe, Sydney, NSW 2037
Britain (and Europe, Africa, and the Middle East):
    Pathfinder, 47 The Cut, London, SE1 8LL
Canada:
    Pathfinder, 6566, boul. St-Laurent, Montréal, Québec, H2S 3C6
Iceland:
    Pathfinder, Klapparstíg 26, 2d floor, 121 Reykjavík
New Zealand:
    Pathfinder, 157a Symonds Street, Auckland
Sweden:
    Pathfinder, Vikingagatan 10, S-113 42, Stockholm
United States (and Caribbean and Latin America):
    Pathfinder, 410 West Street, New York, NY 10014

CONTENTS

Introduction   1

  I The Split   6

 II The Transition Period   22

III Radicalism   26

IV Allies and Alliances   40

 V Separatism and Black Nationalism   52

VI Organization   70

VII Malcolm and His Critics   82

Appendix A: Statement of Basic Aims and Objectives, Organization of Afro-American Unity, June 28, 1964   105

Appendix B: Basic Unity Program, Organization of Afro-American Unity, February 15, 1965   113

Appendix C: The Rustin-Kahn Attack, by Robert Vernon   125

Appendix D: Two Interviews, by Jack Barnes   135

Appendix E: On the First Anniversary of Malcolm X's Death, by George Breitman   141

Notes   153

Related Reading   157

Related Listening   167

INTRODUCTION

The present work is partly the outgrowth of another book, *Malcolm X Speaks,* which I helped to prepare for publication.

In January, 1965, George Novack, acting as a representative of Merit Publishers, visited Malcolm X in his Harlem office to propose the publication of a collection of his speeches, especially from the period after his withdrawal from the Black Muslims. Malcolm responded favorably to the idea, but put off a decision until after he had a chance to consult with the agent handling his forthcoming autobiography. He told Novack that one thing he would want included in the collection, even though it was not a speech, was the text of the memorandum he had submitted to the Organization of African Unity at its meeting in Cairo in July, 1964.

Malcolm was assassinated on February 21, 1965, before any further steps were taken toward publication of his speeches. Believing that the book was now needed more than before, Merit Publishers invited an associate of Malcolm, who had been present at the original discussion, to edit the collection, select the contents and introduce them. He agreed, and began to gather tapes of Malcolm's speeches and written texts, where available.

Unfortunately, his other responsibilities severely limited the time he had to edit the speeches, so the publishers asked me to collaborate with him as co-editor. I had never met Malcolm or even heard him speak in person, but I did have a keen interest in what he had been trying to do during the last year of his life, and I had given the first comprehensive speech about him after his death.* With the

---

* This was published as a pamphlet, *Malcolm X: The Man and His Ideas* (Pioneer Publishers, March, 1965). Some of its material has been incorporated into this book.

concurrence of Malcolm's associate, I accepted the invitation.

After the tapes and written material had been collected and examined, we agreed on a tentative table of contents, and the transcription of the tapes began in April. Because of his other commitments, it was agreed that I would prepare the first drafts of the prefatory notes introducing the various speeches.

In my memorial speech I had tried to call attention to certain patterns which I thought, on the basis of the scanty evidence then available to me, could be detected in the evolution of Malcolm's ideas during 1964-65. Now, as I went over to the tapes of almost twenty full speeches from that period, I realized, with growing excitement, that these patterns were indisputable. Nobody, apparently, had *fully* understood the trend of Malcolm's thought while he was alive, except himself. No one but he had been present on all the occasions when he gave these speeches, and most of them had not been transcribed and printed before his death. Malcolm himself had not had the opportunity to put the parts together – he was under intense pressure all the time, exhausted most of the time, and aware that he might not have much time left.

I therefore had a strong urge, while writing the prefatory notes to the various speeches, to comment on them – to discuss the significance of Malcolm's statements about this or that question, and how they differed from, developed, went beyond or related to what he said about it on previous or subsequent occasions.

But I quickly learned that my co-editor had different opinions from mine. Like some other members of the Muslim Mosque, Inc., he believed that it had been a serious mistake for Malcolm to "go into politics" in his last year; he thought Malcolm should have restricted himself to the religious sphere and concentrated on building the Muslim Mosque, Inc.

Since our opinions were incompatible, we agreed to omit virtually all interpretative comment from the foreword and prefatory notes of *Malcolm X Speaks,* leaving them as factual and objective as possible.

Then, just as the editorial work on the book was being

completed in June, Malcolm's associate felt that he had to withdraw from the project, and I was left as the sole editor. I would have liked at that point to revise and expand my editorial notes, but the publishers wanted to get the book out as soon as possible and would not wait. So they were printed in their original form.

The present work, a year later, is an expanded version of what I would have liked to do in the notes to Malcolm's speeches (it also contains material I did not have access to at that time). I think that *Malcolm X Speaks* speaks for itself. An attentive reader can derive from it most of the conclusions that are presented in this work. What I have tried to do here is make it easier to grasp the connections and implications of the various parts.

The Last Year of Malcolm X was also stimulated by the publication of *The Autobiography of Malcolm X* toward the end of 1965. The *Autobiography* is a very valuable work, indispensable for those who want to understand Malcolm, and Grove Press deserves thanks for publishing it after Doubleday, which had commissioned its writing, abandoned it following Malcolm's assassination. But while it contains much material not available elsewhere, it is not the definitive work on Malcolm that it might have been.

Malcolm was not a writer; he told his autobiography to Alex Haley. Because Haley did not sympathize with his views, Malcolm stipulated that nothing be in the book that he had not said and that nothing be left out that he wanted in it. The actual writing and arrangement of the material were done by Haley. As Malcolm had predicted, he did not live to read the full and final version; he was killed on the weekend when he had planned to visit Haley's home for a final reading of the manuscript.

Haley appears to have honored Malcolm's stipulation to the best of his ability and understanding, but his political understanding was, as I. F. Stone put it, "conventional." Even after the split he did not fully grasp the changes in Malcolm's outlook which took place with great speed in the final months, and the book does not adequately reflect these changes.

The total effect is somewhat blurred, furthermore, because

originally this was to be the story of Malcolm the Black Muslim; the first dedication was to Elijah Muhammad and the royalties were to go to his organization. It was begun early in 1963, a full year before Malcolm's break with the Black Muslims in March, 1964, and a large part, perhaps most, of the material was told and written down before the split. If it had been published then, it would still have been a fascinating narrative, but along strictly "orthodox" Black Muslim lines. *

After the split with Muhammad and Malcolm's first trip abroad in the spring of 1964, he and Haley added some material to the book; and in December, 1964, after his second, longer trip to Africa, they added a little more. Only the report of the split and Malcolm's first trip to Mecca and Africa can be regarded as adequate. His second and longer trip gets very little space, and there is almost nothing in Malcolm's part of the *Autobiography* about the crucial last three months of his life, which was when his ideas were developing most rapidly.

Despite the thousand other things he was trying to do, Malcolm wanted to make changes in the book, beginning soon after the split. He let Haley talk him out of it. Haley reports in his epilogue that Malcolm would "frown and wince" as he read the parts of the manuscript Haley let him see, but in the end he kept his word to Haley and did not insist on rewriting. Haley says that Malcolm wanted to alter or delete favorable statements about Muhammad, and there is no reason to doubt that this was part of what Malcolm wanted to change. But since we know about the new ideas that Malcolm was beginning to express publicly, especially after May, 1964 – ideas that were at variance with some written earlier for the *Autobiography*, and not just ideas about Muhammad, but political ideas – it is likely that Malcolm also wanted to revise some of the general formulations and even concepts which are so presented in

---

* A condensed version of an early draft of the *Autobiography* was printed in the *Saturday Evening Post* of September 12, 1964. At a meeting in Paris on November 23, when Malcolm was asked a question about a passage in this version concerning Black Muslim doctrine, he said, "It was wrongly worded by the writer" [Haley]. (*Présence Africaine*, English edition, Number 2, 1965)

the *Autobiography* that they can be mistaken for the ideas of his last months, which they no longer were. In his epilogue Haley does in at least one place what Malcolm probably wanted to do in many; he quotes the position on intermarriage that Malcolm adopted toward the end of his life, which was radically different from the one expressed in the middle of the book. But a gap remains in the work as a whole on other, more basic questions.

Consequently, the *Autobiography*, even with Haley's long epilogue, is politically incomplete, and in some ways ambiguous or misleading (as in the insertion in the last chapter, entitled "1965," of a paragraph about revolution that clearly belongs to an earlier phase of Malcolm's development). The present work is, in part, an effort to add what is missing or muted in the *Autobiography* and to clarify some of the ambiguities, thus providing the basis for a balanced judgment.

The Last Year of Malcolm X is dedicated to the young black freedom fighters of our country, whom Malcolm counted on to lead their people in a successful struggle for equality. They already know or sense that Malcolm was an incorruptible and uncompromising revolutionary. They can only benefit from learning more about the ideas he had reached and the problems he was still grappling with at the time of his death.

Detroit, Michigan
June, 1966

I. THE SPLIT

It is not possible to fully understand the evolution of Malcolm X in the last year of his life without knowing where he stood at the beginning of that year. The place to start is with the nature and causes of the split in the Black Muslim movement, which came to a head in March, 1964.

The Black Muslims reached Malcolm at a time of acute crisis in his life: A young man in his twenties, he was in prison (1946-52), alone, rebellious, groping to understand what had happened to him and where he fitted into the future. A movement denouncing white oppression had enormous appeal to him because he felt he had been a victim of that oppression; he knew he would not have received an excessive 10-year sentence for burglary the first time he was convicted if he had not flouted white-supremacist morality by having a white girl-friend as an accomplice.

Perhaps a non-religious movement of the right type might have recruited him at that time – but none came into touch with him then, and the Black Muslims did. It was a religious conversion because the answers he was searching for were supplied by a religious movement; he embraced its religious along with its non-religious aspects. But its main attraction for him was its message that he had sunk to the depths because of white oppression and that the Nation of Islam provided a vehicle to combat and end that oppression. As Robert Vernon has pointed out:

> In addition to the usual comforts of religious spirituality, the Nation of Islam had developed a slashing indictment of Christianity on a religious-political basis which struck home to many black people, utilizing the very Bible of the Christians to illustrate in vivid terms the hell the black

man was experiencing in America. (The Islamic or pseudo-Islamic ritual was entirely irrelevant to this process. So long as the movement had meaning to the ghetto poor in terms of their own experiences, and provided psychological and material therapy against the ravages of a white-dominated hell called America, the religion could have been Black Buddhism or Black Brahmanism or Black Anything with equal effect.) [1]

Despite his conversion in prison and his adherence to religion until his death, religion was not the dominant concern of Malcolm's thought or activity during or after his Black Muslim days. In the spring of 1964, following his return from Mecca, where he had become a follower of orthodox Islam, he said:

> No religion will ever make me forget the conditions of our people in this country. No religion will ever make me forget the continued fighting with dogs against our people in this country. No religion will ever make me forget the police clubs that come up 'side our heads. No God, no religion, no nothing will make me forget it until it stops, until it's finished, until it's eliminated. I want to make that point clear. [2]

And he told a rally of the Organization of Afro-American Unity in the fall of 1964, after a long stay in Africa and the Middle East:

> Any time I have a religion that won't let me fight for my people, I say to hell with that religion. That's why I'm a Muslim. [3]

Did Malcolm really believe "Yacub's History" (of how the white race was created as an inferior offshoot of the black) and the rest of the Black Muslim demonology? Did he really think Elijah Muhammad had been appointed by God or a representative of God? Perhaps at the start he did believe these claims, which he repeated obediently when he became a Black Muslim minister. But it is certain that before the split with Muhammad he had come to regard them as symbolic rather than literal truths, or as useful weapons in the struggle against the enemy rather than truths.

Did he, after becoming a Black Muslim leader, traveling widely and mixing in new circles, continue to believe that the Black Muslims were an orthodox Islamic grouping, or that, as Muhammad taught, no white could be a Muslim? It is likely that these were among the questions that he tried not to think about. (Shutting out of his mind problems that he didn't feel could be solved was "one of the characteristics I don't like about myself," he told Alex Haley.[4])

In any case, these were not issues raised by Malcolm or Muhammad at the time of the split, and religious differences, although they developed after the split, were not its cause.

Of Malcolm's unswerving devotion and loyalty to Muhammad during the years when he was a Black Muslim (1952-64), there can be no doubt. Muhammad himself publicly recognized this in 1963 when he appointed Malcolm as the first "national minister" of the Nation of Islam. Malcolm was not exaggerating when he said he would have laid down his life for Muhammad without hesitation. Through Muhammad, he said,

> the religion of Islam had reached down into the mud to lift me up, to save me from being what I inevitably would have been: a dead criminal in a grave, or, if still alive, a flint-hard, bitter, thirty-seven-year-old convict in some penitentiary, or insane asylum. Or, at best, I would have been an old, fading Detroit Red, hustling, stealing enough for food and narcotics, and myself being stalked as prey by cruelly ambitious younger hustlers such as Detroit Red had been. [5]

Muhammad not only helped to save Malcolm from degradation and self-destruction, he also trained him and made it possible for him to utilize his talents and energies constructively in behalf of his people:

> I had helped Mr. Muhammad and his other ministers to revolutionize the American black man's thinking, opening his eyes until he would never again look in the same fear-

ful, worshipful way at the white man. I had participated in spreading the truths that had done so much to help the American black man rid himself of the mirage that the white race was made up of "superior" beings. [6]

In the beginning of their relationship, Muhammad was the teacher and Malcolm the pupil. Quick to see Malcolm's exceptional abilities, Muhammad soon gave him greater responsibilities and latitude than his other ministers. Looking back after the split, Malcolm said that in those days he had spoken, thought and acted through the mind of Muhammad, rather than his own; he even used the term "zombie." But this was something of an exaggeration. Malcolm's mind was too keen, his interests too broad, for him to be a mere parrot.

He stretched the bounds of Muhammad's doctrine to the limit, and sometimes beyond. He introduced new elements into the movement, not only of style but of ideology: There was more than a grain of truth in the complaint made by James X, who replaced Malcolm as head of the New York Black Muslim mosque after the split, and his assistant, Henry X, that "it was Malcolm who injected the political concept of 'black nationalism' into the Black Muslim movement, which they said was essentially religious in nature when Malcolm became a member." [7] But it is also true that Malcolm never deliberately did anything he thought Muhammad would disapprove, and that he really wanted to be what he constantly called himself—"Mr. Muhammad's representative."

Thus, although there was an element of undisciplined behavior on Malcolm's part in the incident leading to the split, it was not a main or central cause.

In the *Autobiography* appears the statement: "Mr. Muhammad and I are not together today only because of envy and jealousy." [8] There is no reason to doubt that Malcolm said this to Alex Haley in just those words some time during the second year of the period when the *Autobiography* was being written, or that Malcolm believed it when he said it. But it is not an accurate or adequate explanation, and it does not reflect the opinion Malcolm had reached about the split before his death. (And it is another example of how Haley's insistence that Malcolm not revise certain parts of the *Autobiography* creates unnecessary confusion.)

This is not to deny that personal factors played a part in the Black Muslim split. Malcolm's conclusion toward the end of 1962 that Muhammad had been violating the strict sexual code prescribed for all members of the movement undoubtedly weakened his respect for Muhammad. Muhammad's confidence in Malcolm was probably eroded by the slanderous rumors about Malcolm that were circulated by members of the Muhammad family circle in Chicago who feared that their positions and privileges in the national staff of the movement might be endangered if Malcolm succeeded Muhammad when the latter died or retired from active leadership.

Personal factors play a part in every organizational crisis and split. It is hard to think of any mass movement, past or present, that has been free of personal differences and antagonisms. These inevitably become more pronounced when a movement is confronted with the possibility of a split. To leading participants, caught up in the passions of an internal struggle, personal factors may appear to be the "only" cause of a split, or the main cause. But that is rarely the case. And it was not the case with the split in the Nation of Islam.

The occasion for the split was a remark made by Malcolm at a New York meeting on December 1, 1963, nine days after the assassination of President Kennedy. In answer to a question from the floor, Malcolm attributed Kennedy's death to the climate of hate and violence that white people had created or tolerated: "chickens come home to roost."* It was in line with pronouncements that the Black Muslims had been making for years – that God was punishing white Americans for their crimes against blacks. But Muhammad had given strict orders to all his ministers not to make any comment on the assassination, and technically Malcolm was guilty of a violation of discipline.

---

* The account that appears in the *Autobiography* does not mention that Malcolm added: "Being an old farm boy myself, chickens coming home to roost never did make me sad; they've always made me glad." 9

The next day Malcolm went to Chicago for his regular monthly meeting with Muhammad. "That was a very bad statement," Muhammad told him. "The country loved this man. The whole country is in mourning. That was very ill-timed. A statement like that can make it hard on Muslims in general." His verdict: "I'll have to silence you for the next ninety days – so that the Muslims everywhere can be disassociated from the blunder."

A public 90-day suspension was humiliating, but did not seem entirely unreasonable. Malcolm answered, "Sir, I agree with you, and I submit, one hundred percent." When questioned by the press on his return to New York, he said the same thing, adding that he expected to be speaking again (reinstated) after ninety days. But it soon became evident that Muhammad had not been candid with him – the "suspension" was indefinite, probably permanent. The members were told that he would be reinstated after ninety days "if he submits." But he had already submitted, privately and publicly; why were the members being given the impression that he had not? Then he heard that one of his assistants was telling certain members, "If you knew what the Minister did, you'd go out and kill him yourself." Malcolm believed that "any death-talk for me could have been approved of – if not actually initiated – by only one man." He came to the conclusion that the "chickens coming home to roost" statement had been only a pretext for putting into action a plan to isolate and remove him altogether from the movement, perhaps even from life. His head "felt like it was bleeding inside . . . I was in a state of emotional shock . . . I felt as though something in *nature* had failed, like the sun, or the stars."[10]

With the approach of the annual Black Muslim convention in Chicago on February 26, 1964, he telephoned Muhammad and asked for a clarification of his status. He got a letter from Muhammad that left the question unanswered. He decided then that the time had come to act. After much soul-searching, he became "able finally to muster the nerve, and the strength, to start facing the facts, to think for myself." On March 8 he announced that he was leaving the Nation of Islam and starting a new organization.

It is instructive to take note of the way in which Muhammad had posed the problem to Malcolm. It wasn't merely
an undisciplined action or blunder – it was a question of
policy. Fearing an adverse public reaction and a possible
government attack on his movement if it made provoca-
tive statements about the assassination, Muhammad, who
was very sensitive to such possibilities, wanted to play
things safe; his newspaper was instructed to join in the
mourning over Kennedy. The more aggressive Malcolm
instinctively sought to extract from the situation every
possible propaganda advantage over the enemy, even if
it involved risks. Differences of personal temperament? Of
course. But along with them, and historically more important, were differences over policy – in this case, over tactics,
over the stance of the movement. Muhammad took the extreme step of breaking with his most valuable lieutenant
because he realized, ahead of Malcolm, how deep the differences were and would become.

Hardly anyone, even in the ghetto, heard of the Black
Muslims during the first quarter-century after their formation in 1931. During that time they remained a small, un-
influential sect in a few cities; their members were mainly
middle-aged or older and their numbers were in the hundreds. In the late 1950s they quickly grew to the tens of
thousands, most of them young; their sympathizers and
admirers were far more numerous, and they became a
center of national attention. This change was produced by
a combination of factors:
1. The spread of the colonial revolution among the non-
white peoples of Asia and Africa stimulated racial pride
in black Americans and the hope that the end of white
supremacy was dawning on a world-wide scale. 2. The national government's failure to enforce the Supreme Court's
1954 decision against school segregation convinced many
black people that they would have to rely on their own
struggles to make progress toward racial equality. 3. A
section of the ruling class, which believed some concessions would have to be given to the Negroes, encouraged
the press and TV to publicize the Black Muslims widely
(and sensationally) as a horrible alternative to "respon-

sible" leaders like Roy Wilkins and Martin Luther King.
4. Malcolm became a leader of the Black Muslims in the
1950s, supplying talents as propagandist and organizer
that proved to be remarkably effective. (Using the same
talents in the different climate and soil of the 1930s or
1940s, it is unlikely that he would have accomplished
much.)

The Black Muslims won mass respect and a following
in the ghetto because they "told the white man off" in bold
and confident tones. They voiced the discontent that the
black masses felt with their lot in this country, with tokenism, gradualism and white hypocrisy. They exposed the
vacillations of the "moderate" Negro leaders, accusing them
of representing the white ruling class more than the black
masses, and by their pressure pushed them to the left, at
least verbally. There were millions of Negroes who would
never join the Black Muslims, but were glad that they
existed.

The Black Muslims operated under a number of handi-
caps that seriously limited their appeal and possibilities of
recruitment. Their discipline was very strict. They demanded
many sacrifices from their members. Their moral and sexual codes were puritanical. The members had many obligations and few rights; no pretense was made that the organization was democratic. Their religion seemed exotic to
Negroes still under the influence of Christianity and bogus
to the few attracted to orthodox Islam, and it was an
obstacle to those who had learned from sad experience to
be wary of rackets disguising themselves as churches. Their
solution – "separation" – was couched in vague terms, hard
to pin down concretely and understand at a non-emotional
level.

In addition, the Black Muslims ran up against a wall
created by their own sectarianism. They were able to ignore it when they first began to expand, but later it produced a crisis.

Their stress on the need for black unity was one of their
main assets, the source of much of their popularity. It
went over big in the late 1950s when the ghetto, especially
in the North, was relatively quiescent. But in 1960 the
students began their sit-ins in the South, initiating a black

upsurge that spread within a few years throughout the South and into the North. By 1962-63 there were demonstrations, marches, picketlines all over the country, many of them on a mass scale and most of them involving or led by young people.

It had been one thing to preach black unity when there was virtually no other force in motion for the Black Muslims to unite with; it became another when they were confronted with a wave of mass actions and, in effect, a demand that they practice what they preached. Previously, the pressure had all been one-way – from the Black Muslims and on the traditional civil rights organizations. Now the Black Muslims began to feel some pressure themselves – for black unity. Though they were "separated" organizationally from the rest of the black community, the Black Muslims could not escape its pressures, especially because they came from the youngest and most militant of the non-Muslims, those whom the Nation of Islam was most interested in attracting.

It was a real dilemma. Muhammad's concept of black unity was unity of blacks inside his movement and under his discipline. But he could not say that openly or directly – it would have been the equivalent of discarding the popular unity slogan. So he kept on talking in favor of black unity. But it was an abstraction; in practice the Black Muslims stayed on the sidelines, watching the action of others.

A dialogue would take place when young activists engaged in a battle for jobs at a construction site. "Integration is a fraud, it is not the solution," Black Muslims would tell them. "Maybe you are right, maybe separation is the answer," the young activists replied, "but what is wrong with our getting some jobs for our people who are unemployed, and why can't you help us do it without giving up your belief that integration will not solve our over-all problem?" The Black Muslims would belittle the smallness of the objective: "Six jobs, ten, twenty – what good will that do?" "It's a beginning – if we win some here, it will encourage our people to fight elsewhere and on a bigger scale; why don't you help us?" "We don't believe in begging the white man, we believe in doing things for ourselves." "But we're not begging – we're demanding, we're fighting. Isn't fighting doing something for yourself? Why don't you give us a hand?" And so on. These discussions lowered the prestige of the Black Muslims in the eyes of the young militants. They also had an effect on the Black Muslims, who answered by rote, but with decreasing conviction.

In various cities throughout 1963 Negro organizations approached Black Muslim ministers and urged them to participate in protest demonstrations. In some cases the ministers themselves rejected the invitations; in others they said they would have to take the matter up with Muhammad (who made many local decisions). In the end the answer always was, "No, we cannot participate." But those ministers who went to Muhammad about this must have thought there was a possibility of getting permission, and some of them must have wanted it. These local ministers were reflecting rank-and-file Black Muslim sentiment to some degree, or they saw the danger of their movement being bypassed and isolated as growing numbers of black people moved into action.

The Black Muslims had been effective as a propaganda group, but the time had come for action as well as talk. Abstention from the action that was unfolding lessened their effectiveness even as a propaganda group by 1963, when Negroes, by the hundreds of thousands, were looking for action to change their conditions—"now," not in the future.

Muhammad maneuvered with the problem, but the areas of maneuver kept getting smaller. At the February, 1963, annual convention in Chicago he came out dramatically for independent black political action and the running of independent black candidates for public office. It was, again, effective propaganda. In the early years of the movement Muhammad could have gone on expounding this theme and reaping benefits from it for a long time, without having to put up. But a mere six months later a group of black militants announced the formation of the Freedom Now Party. Muhammad dropped the issue like a hot stone, and his ministers could only hem and haw when they were asked about joining the Freedom Now Party.

Prior to this, there was an incident that brought out the same problem from another angle. On April 27, 1962, at a time when there was much talk about Washington preparing to crack down on the Black Muslims as "subversive," the Los Angeles police shot seven unarmed Black Muslims in cold blood, killing one and crippling another for life. Then they arrested sixteen of their victims on false charges of "criminal assault against the police" and held them under bail totaling $160,000.

Muhammad dispatched Malcolm to Los Angeles to handle the case. Under his leadership the prisoners were bailed out, lawyers were hired to defend them, mass protest meetings were organized, and the press and TV were forced to give some publicity to the truth about what had happened. Malcolm was struck by the fact that *all* sections of the Negro community joined in the protest against the police atrocity.

This led him to the conclusion that the Los Angeles case should not be viewed as merely a local attack against which defensive measures had to be taken. He saw it as an exceptional opportunity for a counter-attack (under a defensive formula) through which the Black Muslims could win the active aid of black people all over the country. A campaign in defense of the Los Angeles victims and around the issue of police brutality, could, if skillfully and boldly conducted, forge bonds of solidarity and unity between Muslim and non-Muslim Negroes strong enough to discourage or deter government persecution of the Nation of Islam. The whole country could be aroused, he thought; there could be an appeal to the conscience of everyone who had a conscience. Accordingly, in the early literature on the case, even whites were addressed: "Whether you are white or black, this is your fight too. Whites who claim to be liberal, and profess friendship and a desire to right the wrongs done by their people to our people, should give all-out FINANCIAL support in this great struggle against police brutality." In this literature there was also a conscious effort to overcome the barriers of religious sectarianism: "It was a Muslim Mosque this time; next it will be the Protestant Church, the Catholic Cathedral, the Jewish Synagogue."[11]

What Malcolm had in mind, though he did not use the analogies, was something like the mass defense movements organized in behalf of Sacco and Vanzetti in the 1920s and the Scottsboro Boys in the 1930s.

The merits of such an approach were so obvious that the proposed campaign got approval from headquarters in Chicago (that is, Muhammad). Preparations for a big nation-wide campaign were made in the summer of 1962. It was discussed with the ministers and explained to the members—it had to be because it was going to involve the whole movement in something bigger and different than anything it had tried before.

Then, without advance notice and without explanation, the whole thing was called off. The Black Muslim newspaper of course continued to write about the Los Angeles atrocity, but with less space and emphasis. Instead of a mass defense movement, a decision had been made to conduct a purely legal defense in the courts. No united fronts, no mass meetings, no broad agitation—just a court case. Those who persisted with questions were told privately that a mass campaign "would only antagonize the authorities and make it worse for the brothers in court."

This was the first time that some of the rank-and-file members became aware of the existence of at least two tendencies in the leadership. It made some of them ask themselves, "Why is it that Mr. Muhammad not only instructs us not to join non-Muslims on their picketlines but also does not want them to join with us when we are attacked by the police?"

The differences over the Los Angeles case are not mentioned at all in the *Autobiography*.* There the general problem of sectarianism is referred to briefly in two paragraphs added after the split, where Malcolm says, after

---

* But he did refer to them—in strong terms—during a talk in Harlem to a group of young people from McComb, Mississippi, on December 31, 1964. Discussing the summer voter-registration campaign in Mississippi, where "three brothers" had been murdered, he criticized the civil rights organizations for not having protected them and for not reacting properly after the murders. Then he added: "That's what split the Muslim movement. That's what caused the Black Muslim movement to be split. Some of our brothers got hurt, and nothing was done about it, and those of us who wanted to do something about it were kept from doing something about it. So we split."

summing up the positive and satisfying sides to his experiences as a Black Muslim:

> If I harbored any personal disappointment whatsoever, it was that privately I was convinced that our Nation of Islam could be an even greater force in the American black man's over-all struggle – if we engaged in more *action*. By that, I mean I thought privately that we should have amended, or relaxed, our general non-engagement policy. I felt that, wherever black people committed themselves, in the Little Rocks and Birminghams and other places, militantly disciplined Muslims should also be there – for all the world to see, and respect, and discuss.
>
> It could be heard increasingly in the Negro communities: "Those Muslims *talk* tough, but they never *do* anything, unless somebody bothers Muslims." I moved around among outsiders more than most other Muslim officials. I felt the very real potentiality that, considering the mercurial moods of the black masses, this labeling of Muslims as "talk only" could see us, powerful as we were, one day suddenly separated from the Negroes' front-line struggle. [12]

When Malcolm here twice uses the word "privately," he evidently wishes to say that he did not go around sharing these thoughts with non-Muslims or rank-and-file Muslims. That is understandable, given the bureaucratic nature of the organization. Perhaps he also means to convey the idea that he never discussed them with Muhammad. It would be astonishing if that were the case, or if Muhammad on his own had never raised these questions with his chief lieutenant; astonishing, but not impossible, given a one-man leadership (the one man being an emissary from God at that). But the whole passage has an unsatisfactory ring. Notice how delicately the problem is put: "our general non-engagement policy." And notice too that the problem that was plaguing the Black Muslims long before the split is here referred to only as a "potentiality."

Malcolm spoke much more plainly about the problem soon after his suspension in December, 1963, when he was interviewed by Louis Lomax. This was before he had decided that there was no longer any place for him in the Nation of Islam. Malcolm denied heatedly that there were even minor differences between himself and Muhammad.

But then he went on to add something that surprised Lomax because it was the first time he had ever heard Malcolm deviate from Muhammad on anything.

> . . . But I will tell you this: The Messenger [Muhammad] has seen God. He was with Allah and was given divine patience with the devil. He is willing to wait for Allah to deal with the devil. Well, sir, the rest of us Black Muslims have not seen God, we don't have this gift of divine patience with the devil. The younger Black Muslims want to see some action. [13]

Though the complaint wears the religious garb of the movement, its meaning is unmistakable: Muhammad is too willing to wait for the enemy to be taken care of – who knows for how long? – but we, the younger Black Muslims, who lack that "gift" for waiting, want to see some action now. When Malcolm spoke these words, it was obviously not a "private" matter – he was reflecting the sentiments of the younger members of his movement, who in turn were reflecting the pressures from non-Muslim militants in the ghetto.

No "factions" were tolerated in the Black Muslims; people were not permitted to band together in organized groupings to push for this or that change of policy. But there were different tendencies just the same. Without anybody ever saying it out loud, it was understood or sensed in the years before the split that Malcolm represented the activist, radical tendency in the leadership, and Muhammad the abstentionist, conservative tendency. The differences between these tendencies shaped the split.

By March 8, 1964, Malcolm had made up his mind. Religious terminology was cast aside, the previous restraints were lifted, and he publicly stated that the Black Muslim movement "had 'gone as far as it can' because it was too narrowly sectarian and too inhibited":

> "I am prepared," Malcolm said, "to cooperate in local civil rights actions in the South and elsewhere and shall do so because every campaign for specific objectives can only heighten the political consciousness of the Negroes and intensify their identification against white society." . . .
> "There is no use deceiving ourselves," Malcolm said.

"Good education, housing and jobs are imperatives for Negroes, and I shall support them in their fight to win these objectives, but I shall tell the Negroes that while these are necessary, they cannot solve the main Negro problem."

Malcolm continued:

"I shall also tell them that what has been called the 'Negro revolution' in the United States is a deception practiced upon them, because they have only to examine the failure of this so-called revolution to produce any positive results in the past year.

"I shall tell them what a real revolution means – the French Revolution, the American Revolution, Algeria, to name a few. There can be no revolution without bloodshed, and it is nonsense to describe the civil rights movement in America as a revolution." . . .

Malcolm said Elijah Muhammad had prevented him from participating in civil rights struggles in the South although he had had many opportunities to do so.

"It is going to be different now," Malcolm said. "I'm going to join in the fight wherever Negroes ask for my help, and I suspect my activities will be on a greater and more intensive scale than in the past." 14

In the same statement Malcolm also said that "jealousy and personal rivalry were responsible for his suspension," but the nature of his statement as a whole reduced these factors to their properly subordinate position. They did not, could not, explain why Malcolm was preparing to build a different kind of movement than the one he was leaving – a movement that would join and support all struggles for partial and limited objectives (in contrast to the Black Muslims*) at the same time that it would promote understanding of a "real revolution" to solve the "main problem" (in contrast to the traditional civil rights organizations).

---

* Since this is an examination of Malcolm's evolution and not that of the Black Muslims, a few words about the latter will have to do. Only a few Black Muslims left with Malcolm. A larger number dropped out during the following year, but not enough to cripple the organization. Nevertheless, Malcolm's withdrawal had a devastating effect on the Nation of Islam. As long as the tendency he represented played a part in the leadership, the Black Muslims had a potential for resolving their contradictions in a progressive direction. Before he left,

Thus there is a pattern, a certain symmetry, in Malcolm's evolution. Before becoming a Black Muslim, he had been alienated from his people as well as white society. He was attracted to the Black Muslims because they gave him a sense of identification with his people and an organization through which to advance their interests as well as his own. Traveling all over the country as Muhammad's lieutenant, he had got to know the people in the ghetto better than anyone else. In fact, he came – before he was fully conscious of it himself – to identify with the black masses more than with the Nation of Islam; under the impact of the Negro upsurge of the 1960s, he began to put their needs ahead of the interests of the Black Muslim hierarchy. The suspension compelled him to open his mind to realities he had been shutting out. It drove him to the conclusion that the Nation of Islam had "gone as far as it can"; he intended to go much further. As a Black Muslim he had rejected American society; now he began to move toward action to change society. He left the Black Muslims for essentially the same reason he had joined them – because he wanted to fight for the freedom of his people.

---

many thousands of independent black militants and radicals had counted strongly on the possibility that the Black Muslims might join the broader freedom struggle and help to transform it. With his departure, a qualitative change took place both inside the Nation of Islam and in its relations with the rest of the black community. Its dynamism withered, its morale fell; and so did its public standing. (This happened before Malcolm's assassination.) By breaking with Malcolm, Muhammad had made his decision – to keep his organization "separate" from black militancy as well as white society. The price of this decision was that the Black Muslims cut themselves off from the opportunity of becoming a significant part of the coming black revolution.

II. THE TRANSITION PERIOD

The split with the Black Muslims took Malcolm by surprise – he was not prepared for it psychologically, ideologically or organizationally. Psychological readjustment, though painful, came fastest; in the other areas he needed more time and experience. He had to do more than merely reject attitudes, ideas and methods long held as a Black Muslim – he had to sift them, retaining some and revising others, and he had to add new ones.

It is one thing to declare independence, another to be able to develop a perspective, philosophy and movement aiming at revolutionary changes in society. In a situation where he was surrounded by more pressures and enemies than before, Malcolm now had to do the hardest thing in the world – think for himself. Previously he had been able to "shut his mind" to certain difficult questions (the privilege of a lieutenant); as a leader he had to confront them, ready or not. Historical precedent for what he wanted to do was meager or unknown to him, and he did not get much theoretical help from the few Black Muslims who joined him at the outset; they were dedicated, but less experienced than he was.

The brief independent phase of Malcolm's life (only 50 weeks, half of which were spent abroad) really divides into two distinct parts. The first was a transition period, which lasted around two or three months, from the split early in March to his return from Africa at the end of May, 1964. A great deal of confusion about what Malcolm stood for and where he was moving can be avoided by clearly distinguishing this transition period from the final period (June, 1964, to February, 1965).

In this transition period Malcolm inevitably made mistakes. He made some false starts and had to retrace his steps. He said and did things which he himself later called errors; in other cases he did not publicly call them errors but he changed positions he had taken in the transition period.

An example of the first can be found in the *Saturday Evening Post* version of the *Autobiography* (September 12, 1964): Hoping to avoid conflict with the Black Muslims, Malcolm originally decided not to make his criticisms of Muhammad public; if he had spoken out, the split would have been sharper but it would also have been bigger, and Muhammad might have had fewer resources with which to attack him. Looking back in the summer of 1964, when he felt no truce between them was possible, Malcolm said: "I made an error, I know now, in not speaking out the full truth when I was first 'suspended.'"

An example of a position changed between the transition and final periods was in Malcolm's attitude toward white supporters of the freedom struggle. In April a white pacifist minister was killed by a bulldozer during a Cleveland demonstration against school segregation. At a New York meeting James Wechsler of the *New York Post* and other liberals demanded that Malcolm pay tribute to the slain minister, and he refused:

> . . . Good, what the man did is good. But the day is out when you'll find black people who are going to stand up and applaud the contributions of whites at this late date. . . . Don't you ever think I would use my energies applauding the sacrifice of an individual white man. No, that sacrifice is too late. [1]

But in December Malcolm did not need any prodding to praise the two white and one Negro civil rights workers who had been murdered for their voter-registration activities in Mississippi during the summer. If the Cleveland death had occurred during the final period, there is no doubt that Malcolm's response would have been different, and more effective.

The reader who is trying to understand Malcolm's development would therefore do well, when he comes across any passage – in the *Autobiography,* in *Malcolm X Speaks,* or anywhere else – always to ask himself: "Is this from Malcolm's Black Muslim period, is it from the transition period, or is it from the final period?" This will not solve all the problems about contradictory or inconsistent statements, but it will help considerably. It will help, among other things, to expose the dishonesty or ignorance of commentators and critics who insist on lumping all the periods together.

It will surely help to clarify Malcolm's position on such relatively simple questions as interracial marriage. As a Black Muslim, he said that intermarriage was harmful, evil, a device to undermine the freedom struggle. In the transition period, his main emphasis was on the points that intermarriage was difficult and painful for interracial couples "in a world as color-hostile as this," and that it did not "prove anything positive." (His remarks on the subject[2] in the *Autobiography* evidently date from the transition period.) Yet before those remarks from the transition period could be published, he said, on a Canadian TV program a month before his death, that he regarded intermarriage as a personal matter – "it's just one human being marrying another human being," another of the "strides toward oneness" – adding that he did not feel on the defensive about having had different positions in the past, since those earlier positions had been "reactions" by a victim of a discriminatory society.[3]

There were other questions, more complex than intermarriage, where Malcolm did not get the time to follow his thinking to its probable conclusions. But even with these it is helpful to bear in mind the transition period and to avoid mixing it up with the period that followed, where Malcolm's thought reached its most militant and most mature level.

Two other precautions can be recommended in approaching Malcolm's statements during both the transition and final periods. One concerns the relations between Malcolm and the people who interviewed him. Most of them were hostile; he sensed this immediately, and it affected the way he responded. (See Appendix D for Jack Barnes' article, "Two Interviews," which contrasts Malcolm's answers to friendly representatives of the *Young Socialist* with those he gave to the antagonistic liberal, Robert Penn Warren.)

In addition, as Malcolm confessed, he had become guilty at times of giving sensationalist answers to reporters; he himself was partly responsible for his distorted image in the press, he told Marlene Nadle:

> The reporters came with preconceived answers to their questions. They were looking for sensationalism for something that would sell papers, and I gave it to them. If they had asked probing intelligent questions, they would have gotten different answers. [4]

Malcolm was learning to control this tendency after the split, but had not fully mastered it at his death.

The reader must also make allowances for the conditions under which many of Malcolm's statements were made, and the effects these conditions had on how they were formulated. Frank Kofsky, reviewing *Malcolm X Speaks,* correctly notes that

> not . . . every detail of Malcolm's political philosophy has been elaborated with absolute clarity in his speeches . . . Given the work-horse schedule of Malcolm's final months and the absence of any opportunity for sustained reflection, one must expect that here and there an occasional solecism, murky generalization, or even self-contradiction will crop up. But these minor lapses are to be found in the rhetoric of anyone who speaks extemporaneously with the frequency that Malcolm did during those hectic days; they are entirely inconsequential in comparison with the overall tendency of Malcolm's thinking, which must impinge upon even the most casual reader of these addresses with unmistakable force. [5]

III. RADICALISM

After the split with the Black Muslims, Malcolm noted:

> Largely, the American white man's press refused to convey that I was now attempting to teach Negroes a new direction. [1]

> One of the major troubles that I was having in building the organization that I wanted – an all-black organization whose ultimate objective was to help create a society in which there could exist honest white-black brotherhood – was that my earlier public image, my old so-called "Black Muslim" image, kept blocking me. I was trying to gradually reshape that image. I was trying to turn a corner, into a new regard by the public, especially Negroes . . [2]

Alex Haley relates that the last time he saw Malcolm alive, early in January, 1965:

> He talked about the pressures on him everywhere he turned, and about the frustrations, among them that no one wanted to accept anything relating to him except "my old 'hate' and 'violence' image." He said "the so-called moderate" civil rights organizations avoided him as "too militant" and the "so-called militants" avoided him as "too moderate." "They won't let me turn the corner!" he once exclaimed, "I'm caught in a trap!" [3]

Why did the press refuse to convey Malcolm's "new direction"? Why didn't the moderate Negro leaders welcome it? The answer cannot be found in the introduction to the *Autobiography* by M. S. Handler, whose objective reporting of Malcolm's activities in the *New York Times* had won Malcolm's respect. At the end of Malcolm's life, according to Handler, "He no longer inveighed against the United

States but against a segment of the United States represented by overt white supremacists in the South and covert
white supremacists in the North."[4] If that was all, then why
didn't the press and the Negro leadership accept him as a
convert to their viewpoint and make use of him accordingly?

The truth is that they understood (as the ultra-left so-
called militants did not) that the corner Malcolm wanted to
turn was to the left, not the right. They believed that the
"new" Malcolm could pose a greater threat to the status
quo than the Black Muslim Malcolm. In this they were
correct. Though he did not describe himself that way, Malcolm was a radical both before and after leaving the Black
Muslims. After, he was a revolutionary – increasingly anti-
capitalist and pro-socialist as well as anti-imperialist. These
labels fitted, even though he did not apply them to himself.

As a teen-ager, shortly after he came to Harlem early in
World War II, Malcolm once attended a "rent-raising" party,
where canvassers tried to sell the Communist Party's *Daily
Worker,* but it made little impression on him. This seems to
have been the only kind of contact he had with radicals
before he joined the Black Muslims. By the time he became
an auto worker in Detroit after his release from prison,
McCarthyism was in full swing, and radicals of all vari-
eties were on the defensive or in retreat; but by then he
was already a Black Muslim and wouldn't have paid them
attention anyway.

In joining the Black Muslims, Malcolm believed that he
was dedicating himself to a struggle to the end against
white racist society. Even though this struggle took a pre-
dominantly abstentionist form and was in the beginning
completely non-political, for Malcolm it represented a conscious rejection of American society and values. The correct name for that kind of commitment is radical, despite
the failure of most radical organizations to understand
this.

Many of Muhammad's ministers, their attention turned
inward to their organization and away from the society
outside, remained oblivious of politics – conservative, liberal or radical. For a man with Malcolm's thirst for knowledge, this was not possible. Besides, as he became Muham-

mad's chief spokesman to the outside world, he had to learn something about the views of contending movements and ideologies, if only to be able to counter their arguments.

What he learned about such organizations as the Communist Party and the Socialist Party did not make him friendly. Both were hostile to the Black Muslims and repeated slanders against them. Both were blind to the progressive aspects of black nationalism, which, like the liberals, they equated with "racism in reverse." Both were uncritical supporters of the Martin Luther King type of leadership, and both advocated that Negroes should unite with their "lesser-evil" enemies in Democratic Party "coalition" politics. To Malcolm, their policies were indistinguishable from those of the liberals who instructed Negroes that, as a minority, they had to confine their struggle within a framework acceptable to the liberals. If that was "socialism," Malcolm of course wanted no part of it.

One exception was Malcolm's attitude to *The Militant,* the weekly newspaper expressing the views of the Socialist Workers Party. While he was still a Black Muslim, Malcolm used to buy this paper when it was sold outside meetings where he spoke. Even at that time, he said after the split, he used to tell Negroes it was a good paper and they ought to read it. Initially he was attracted to *The Militant* because it sought to explain the Black Muslims and black nationalism and defended them against reactionary distortion and attack. He was drawn closer when he saw that, unlike most radical publications, it did not try to convince black people to subordinate their struggle to the government, the Democratic Party, the labor movement or anything else.

As a Black Muslim, Malcolm was prohibited from having any relations, formal or informal, with radical organizations containing white members. When the split occurred, there was curiosity, naturally, about the attitude he would take to such organizations. William Worthy, who was present at the March 12, 1964, press conference where Malcolm declared his independence of the Black Muslims, reported:

In an exchange with a British reporter, Malcolm refused

to rule out acceptance of possible Communist support. He
resorted to one of his familiar parable-type responses to
avoid a direct yes-or-no answer.

"Let me tell you a little story. It's like me being in a
wolf's den. The wolf sees someone on the outside who is
interested in freeing me from the den. The wolf doesn't
like that person on the outside. But I don't care who opens
that door and lets me out."

"Then your answer is yes?"

"No," replied Malcolm, grinning. "I'm talking about a
wolf." 5

One week later Malcolm was interviewed by A. B. Spellman, the young poet and jazz critic:

Spellman: Do you intend to collaborate with such other
groups as labor unions or socialist groups or any other
groups?

Malcolm X: We will work with anybody who is sincerely
interested in eliminating injustices that Negroes suffer at
the hands of Uncle Sam.

Spellman: What is your evaluation of the civil rights
movement at this point?

Malcolm X: It has run its – it's at the end of its leash.

Spellman: What groups do you consider most promising?

Malcolm X: I know of no group that is promising unless
it's radical. If it's not radical it is in no way involved
effectively in the present struggle. 6

Not long after, around the end of March, Malcolm was
interviewed by Carlos E. Russell, a member of the editorial
board of *Liberator:*

"Speaking of Socialism," I said, "with cybernetics and
automation, last year over 200,000 people were left without jobs. How come neither you nor any of the other
leaders ever use the term Socialism as an alternative?"

Malcolm replied, "Why speak of it! If you want someone
to drink from a bottle, you never put the skull and cross-
bones on the label, for they won't drink. The same is true
here." 7

On April 8, Malcolm spoke on "The Black Revolution" at
the Militant Labor Forum in New York.⁸ This was the first

of three speeches he gave under the auspices of the Militant
Labor Forum in the last year of his life, and the beginning
of an increasingly friendly relationship with American revolutionary socialists.* But Malcolm's interest in socialism
was not stimulated primarily by Americans – it came to
him mainly from abroad.

On April 13 he left for Mecca and Africa, where he spent
around five weeks. The Mecca experience is rather fully
reported in the *Autobiography;* the African account there
is briefer. He kept a diary, and was thinking of using this
material for another book. From subsequent statements it
is plain that his discussions with various people in Africa
on this trip, and on the longer one made later in the year,
had as big an impact on his political thinking as his experiences in Mecca had on his ideas about race and racism.
This is one of the important points that Truman Nelson
misses in his sympathetic review[10] of the *Autobiography*.
He says that after the split with Muhammad, Malcolm "was
drawn off into a tragic diversion: a pilgrimage to Mecca
to prove that he, not Elijah Muhammad, was the real Muslim. This had no relevance to the streets of Harlem." But it
did have enormous relevance to Malcolm and the small

---

* James Farmer's account of this relationship contains almost as many
errors as words. He says: "After he left the Muslims, Malcolm cast this
way and that for a stance. For a while he was strongly influenced by
the Trotskyite Socialist Workers Party which today hopes to prod black
nationalism into violently revolutionary action. But when he traveled
to the Middle East in the fall of 1964, he seemed to be casting about
for some way to join the civil rights movement. 'I have come to this
holy city to worship,' he wrote to me from Mecca. 'In all my years
in the United States, I have never witnessed the brotherhood of man
working as it does here. I've witnessed thousands of pilgrims of all
colors.' He underlined *all colors.*" [9]
Farmer is casting about here for some way to make Malcolm appear
erratic and inconsistent. The truth is that he "wanted to join the civil
rights movement" (that is, enter the active struggle) at the time of the
split, in March, and before then – not in the fall, as Farmer asserts;
this was one of the major reasons for the split. If Farmer would bother
to look at Malcolm's postcard from Mecca, he could see that it was
sent in the spring, not the fall. Farmer is similarly misleading when
he tries to make it seem that Malcolm's friendly relations with the Socialist Workers Party lasted only "for a while." These relations continued throughout Malcolm's last year, and were closer at the end than
at the beginning.

group of ex-Black Muslims who had joined him in the effort to build a new movement. It was a stage in his development that would have been extremely difficult to skip over – in one sense a religious settling of accounts, but in another a differentiation that cleared the ground for other things. The other things included politics, the colonial revolution, and the relation of the American Negro to the world revolution. Nelson mentions the trip to Mecca, but he overlooks the fact that on both of his trips Malcolm spent most of his time not in Mecca and among Muslim religious leaders but in the newly independent African countries and among people with whom he could discuss politics. Later Nelson says that in Malcolm's last months, after his two trips, "He had begun to renew himself, and his regenerated purpose began to take form, a political form. He was talking now like a member of the revolutionary majority." But how can this "regenerated purpose" be fully understood or accounted for without looking to its African sources?

Malcolm's experience had made him skeptical about Americans, including most of those who considered themselves radicals. Speaking to a mixed audience in New York on May 29, 1964, shortly after his first African tour, he said:

> Nowadays, as our people begin to wake up, they're going to realize, they've been talking about Negro revolt, Negro revolution – You can't talk that stuff to me unless you're really for one. And most of you aren't. When the deal goes down, you back out every time." [11]

Speaking to a similar audience on January 7, 1965, after his second African trip, he said that "some changes" would come when whites who were "fed up" learned how to establish the proper type of communication with blacks who were fed up, and then he added:

> But how many sitting here right now feel that they could truly identify with a struggle that was designed to eliminate the basic causes that create the conditions that exist? Not very many. They can jive; but when it comes to identifying yourself with a struggle that is not endorsed

by the power structure, that is not acceptable, where the
ground rules are not laid down by the society which you
live in and which you're struggling against – you can't
identify with that, you step back.

Oh, when things get bad enough, everybody gets into the
act. And that's what is coming – in 1965. 12

In the same speech, Malcolm pointed to the deeply-rooted
cause for such unreliability – the powerfully conservatizing
and corrupting influences exerted by the American economic
and social atmosphere:

You can cuss out colonialism, imperialism, and all other
kinds of ism, but it's hard for you to cuss that dollarism.
When they drop those dollars on you, your soul goes. 13

In Africa Malcolm had the opportunity to mingle with
revolutionaries, both black and white. He was more receptive to their ideas and arguments than those of Americans he knew; he trusted and respected them more. He
called the Algerian ambassador to Ghana, whom he met
in May, "a revolutionary in the true sense of the word
(and has his credentials as such for having carried on a
successful revolution against oppression in his country)";
the Algerian ambassador was white, but he had his credentials. Malcolm was much more ready and willing to
learn from such men than from Americans who might
talk radical talk, but from whom he did not expect much.

When he returned late in May – the transition period ended
approximately here – Malcolm no longer took the skull-
and-crossbones-label attitude to socialism. Volunteering to
speak May 29 at the Militant Labor Forum, he brought
up the subject of socialism himself when he said:

They say travel broadens your scope, and recently I've
had an opportunity to do a lot of it in the Middle East
and Africa. While I was traveling I noticed that most of
the countries that have recently emerged into independence
have turned away from the so-called capitalistic system in
the direction of socialism. So out of curiosity, I can't resist the temptation to do a little investigating wherever

that particular philosophy happens to be in existence or
an attempt is being made to bring it into existence. [14]

Later in that talk he likened capitalism to the chicken:

> It's impossible for a chicken to produce a duck egg —
> even though they both belong to the same family of fowl.
> A chicken just doesn't have it within its system to produce
> a duck egg. It can't do it. It can only produce according
> to what that particular system was constructed to produce.
> The system in this country cannot produce freedom for
> an Afro-American. It is impossible for this system, this
> economic system, this political system, this social system,
> this system, period. It's impossible for this system, as it
> stands, to produce freedom right now for the black man
> in this country.
>
> And if ever a chicken did produce a duck egg, I'm quite
> sure you would say it was certainly a revolutionary
> chicken! [15]

In the question period after his talk Malcolm was asked
what political and economic system he wanted, and he
answered:

> I don't know. But I'm flexible. . . . As was stated earlier,
> all of the countries that are emerging today from under
> the shackles of colonialism are turning toward socialism.
> I don't think it's an accident. Most of the countries that
> were colonial powers were capitalist countries, and the last
> bulwark of capitalism today is America. It's impossible
> for a white person to believe in capitalism and not believe
> in racism. You can't have capitalism without racism. And
> if you find one and you happen to get that person into a
> conversation and they have a philosophy that makes you
> sure they don't have this racism in their outlook, usually
> they're socialists or their political philosophy is socialism.[16]

Another speaker at this May 29 meeting was Clifton De-
Berry, the Socialist Workers Party's presidential candidate
in 1964. In the discussion period Malcolm praised DeBerry's
formulation of the need for a combination of firmness in
principle with flexibility in tactics.

A few weeks later, in a private discussion with DeBerry,

Malcolm said that he sympathized with DeBerry's candidacy and that of course he was not going to support either the Democrats or the Republicans in the election. For various reasons, however, he felt that he could not openly endorse DeBerry. What he could do, he said, was to "open some doors" for DeBerry in Harlem, so that he would get a better hearing for his program and greater circulation of his literature. Malcolm did make such arrangements before his second trip to Africa in July, and before leaving he urged his closest co-workers to cooperate where possible with the Socialist Workers Party's campaign.

Malcolm remained in Africa throughout the 1964 presidential campaign. His attitude to Johnson and Goldwater was expressed in the September 12 *Saturday Evening Post* excerpts from his autobiography:

> Johnson and Goldwater . . . as far as the American black man is concerned, are both just about the same. It's just a question of Johnson, the fox, or Goldwater, the wolf. . . . They both will eat him. [17]

On the way home he stopped off in Paris on November 23 for a speech sponsored by *Présence Africaine,* where he took a crack at "people who call themselves Marxists" and "claim to be enemies of the system," but who were "on their hands and knees" hoping and working for Johnson's election.*

His own anti-capitalist and pro-socialist convictions had become quite strong by this time. He felt the need to express them publicly, not only at socialist meetings but to his own co-workers and supporters in the Organization of Afro-American Unity, most of whom were not socialists and some of whom were anti-socialist. Two months after his final return from Africa, he spoke about this question to Harry Ring, a staff member of *The Militant.* Ring was then giving a series of news commentaries over Station WBAI-FM and had invited Malcolm for an interview that

---

* This was a reference to the American Communist and Socialist parties. On their side, they both remained as antagonistic to Malcolm after he left the Black Muslims as they had been before.

was taped on January 25, 1965, and was broadcast three days later. Ring says:

> While we were waiting for the technical arrangements to be completed at the station, Malcolm expressed his views on some of the problems facing a leader in the mass movement – how to raise the consciousness and understanding of the members without presenting ideas that seemed so far in advance that they would not be acceptable to many in the movement, and how to avoid being labeled in such a way as to become isolated from the ranks.
>
> Malcolm felt it necessary for his people to consider socialist solutions to their problems. But as the leader of a movement, he said, it was necessary to present this concept in a way that would be understandable to his people and would not isolate him from them. It is easy, he commented, for people who are isolated from the movement and who have none of the responsibilities of leadership to stand on the sidelines and make militant-sounding declarations. (This was a reference to an ultra-left publication, *Spartacist,* that had just attacked him as a representative of the World Muslim League who had made his peace with the American power structure.) Most often, he observed, such people simply repeated dogma and were not seriously trying to advance the struggle. [18]

An example of the way Malcolm introduced the concept of socialism to his own followers in Harlem can be found in the speech he made at an OAAU rally at the Audubon Ballroom on December 20, 1964, less than a month after his last return from Africa. The subject of his talk that night was Africa, but before getting to that he said:

> Almost every one of the countries that has gotten independence has devised some kind of socialistic system, and this is no accident. This is another reason why I say that you and I here in America – who are looking for a job, who are looking for better housing, looking for a better education – before you start trying to be incorporated, or integrated, or disintegrated, into this capitalistic system, should look over there and find out what are the people who have gotten their freedom adopting to provide themselves with better housing and better education and better food and better clothing.

None of them are adopting the capitalistic system because they realize they can't. You can't operate a capitalistic system unless you are vulturistic; you have to have
someone else's blood to suck to be a capitalist. You show
me a capitalist, I'll show you a bloodsucker. He cannot
be anything but a bloodsucker if he's going to be a capitalist. He's got to get it from somewhere other than himself, and that's where he gets it – from somewhere or someone other than himself. . . .

There's one thing that Martin Luther King mentioned
at the Armory the other night, which I thought was most
significant. I hope he really understood what he was saying. He mentioned that while he was in some of those
Scandinavian countries he saw no poverty. There was no
unemployment, no poverty. Everyone was getting education, everyone had decent housing, decent whatever-they-
needed-to-exist. But why did he mention those countries
on his list as different?

This is the richest country on earth and there's poverty,
there's bad housing, there's slums, there's inferior education. And this is the richest country on earth. Now, you
know, if those countries that are poor can come up with a
solution to their problems so that there's no unemployment, then instead of you running downtown picketing city
hall, you should stop and find out what they do over there
to solve their problems. This is why the man doesn't want
you and me to look beyond Harlem or beyond the shores
of America. As long as you don't know what's happening
on the outside, you'll be all messed up dealing with this
man on the inside. I mean what they use to solve the problems is not capitalism. What they are using to solve their
problem in Africa and Asia is not capitalism. So what
you and I should do is find out what they are using to
get rid of poverty and all the other negative characteristics
of a rundown society. 19

Eleven days later, in a speech to a delegation of young
civil rights activists from McComb, Mississippi, who spent
their 1964 Christmas vacation in New York City in a trip
sponsored by the Student Nonviolent Coordinating Committee, Malcolm used simple but unequivocal words about
the need to become and stay radical:

You get freedom by letting your enemy know that you'll
do anything to get your freedom; then you'll get it. When

you get that kind of attitude, they'll label you as a "crazy Negro," or they'll call you a "crazy nigger"–they don't say Negro. Or they'll call you an extremist or a subversive, or seditious, or a red or a radical. But when you stay radical long enough, and get enough people to be like you, you'll get your freedom.

By the start of 1965, criticisms and rumors about Malcolm were being circulated around Harlem by both his enemies and some of his friends who could not understand or were unhappy about the course he was following. Alex Haley and Marlene Nadle refer to some of these rumors, but neither mentions the one that charged Malcolm with abandoning black nationalism for "Trotskyism" (a label often applied to *The Militant* and the Socialist Workers Party).

Malcolm continued, at OAAU rallies, to urge the audience to buy *The Militant,* and in opening his speech before the Militant Labor Forum on January 7, 1965, he noted that this was the third time that he had spoken under its auspices:

I always feel that it is an honor and every time that they open the door for me to do so, I will be right here. The *Militant* newspaper is one of the best in New York City. In fact, it is one of the best anywhere you go today.[21]

But he also took the opportunity at this meeting, when he was asked if he would run for mayor of New York under "leftist" sponsorship, to state:

I . . . don't believe that groups should refer to themselves as "leftist," "rightist," or "middle-ist." I think that they should just be whatever they are and don't let people put labels on them–and don't ever put them on yourself. Sometimes a label can kill you. [22]

Though he did not want a label, Malcolm was not at all hesitant about expressing his anti-capitalist position, as in his January 18 interview with the *Young Socialist:*

It is impossible for capitalism to survive, primarily because the system of capitalism needs some blood to suck.

Capitalism used to be like an eagle, but now it's more like a vulture. It used to be strong enough to go and suck anybody's blood, whether they were strong or not. But now it has become more cowardly, like the vulture, and it can only suck the blood of the helpless. As the nations of the world free themselves, then capitalism has less victims, less to suck, and it becomes weaker and weaker. It's only a matter of time in my opinion before it will collapse completely. [23]

Malcolm chuckled when he read this statement after it had been transcribed and submitted to him for any changes he might want to make before publication. Noting that it was the first time he had made such a statement for print, he told Jack Barnes, "This is the farthest I've ever gone. They will go wild over this." (See Appendix D)

The next day, January 19, Malcolm went to Toronto to tape a TV interview for the Pierre Berton Show. One of Berton's questions gave him a chance to state his revised thinking on the nature of the coming world showdown. Earlier—for example, in his talk on "The Black Revolution"[24]—he had stressed the likelihood of a global race war. Now, as he considered the question in the light of his more recent thinking, he applied a different emphasis:

Where an ultimate clash between East and West is concerned, I think that an objective analysis of events that are taking place on this earth today points toward some type of ultimate showdown.

You can call it a political showdown, or even a showdown between the economic systems that exist on this earth, which almost boil down along racial lines. I do believe that there will be a clash between East and West.

I believe that there will ultimately be a clash between the oppressed and those who do the oppressing. I believe that there will be a clash between those who want freedom, justice and equality for everyone and those who want to continue the systems of exploitation. I believe that there will be that kind of clash, but I don't think it will be based upon the color of the skin, as Elijah Muhammad had taught it.

However, I do think that the European powers, which are the former colonial powers, if they're not able to readjust their thinking of superiority toward the darker-skinned people, whom they have been made to think are inferior, then the lines can easily be drawn – they can easily be lumped into racial groups and it will be a racial war. [25]

The same theme was repeated a month later in Malcolm's last formal talk, given at Columbia University on February 18, three days before his death:

We are living in an era of revolution, and the revolt of the American Negro is part of the rebellion against the oppression and colonialism which has characterized this era. . . .

It is incorrect to classify the revolt of the Negro as simply a racial conflict of black against white, or as a purely American problem. Rather, we are today seeing a global rebellion of the oppressed against the oppressor, the exploited against the exploiter. [26]

Truman Nelson calls Malcolm "a man struck down on his way to becoming a revolutionary and a liberator of his people." The material in this chapter indicates that it would be more correct to call him a revolutionary internationalist on the way to becoming a liberator of his people. That is why the American ruling class, the press and the Negro leadership did what they could to prevent him from "turning the corner." That is probably also why he was struck down.

IV.   ALLIES AND ALLIANCES

When Malcolm set out to build a new movement, he had to face the task of working out its relations and attitudes toward other forces in this country and abroad, that is, determine who its allies and potential allies were. A central problem for all movements, racial and national minorities, classes and nations, it is acute for the American Negro people and for any organization that aspires to lead them in the fight for freedom.

Numerically, black people are a minority in the United States (between one-tenth and one-ninth). This creates conditions strategically and tactically different from those in countries where blacks are a majority, and affects both thought and action about allies and alliances. From the fact that Negroes are a minority in the United States many different conclusions can be and are drawn. The one that is most widespread – it was originated by the propagandists for the ruling class, has the blessings of the government, and is accepted and propounded by all the moderate Negro leaders – goes as follows:

Since Negroes are a minority of 10 or 11 percent, the odds are against them. They must recognize that they cannot get equality, or significant concessions in that direction, until they get the acquiescence and support of another 40 percent or more of the nation – whites, who range for the most part from liberal to conservative. Since these whites must be persuaded to support the Negro cause, it follows that Negroes must not antagonize them. That is, Negroes may prod them, but must not push them; Negroes must not be "too unreasonable" or "too radical" in their conduct or demands; Negroes must use only those methods that are acceptable to the whites whom they seek as allies. All-black organization, black leadership, effective self-defense against racist violence, black political action outside the two-party system—these may have strong appeal to the Negro masses, but they are out of the question because white liberals and conservatives do not like them. Anything that smacks of "extremism" or "black nationalism," anything that goes beyond the framework of the "American system" as it is conventionally understood—they too are out. In short, Negroes must go only as far as their liberal-to-conservative white allies are prepared to have them go, only as fast as those allies think they should go, and only under banners that those allies are willing to march under themselves. (Of course those who share this position have differences of opinion over timing, over how much and what kind of prodding is permissible, etc. But in essence they agree that Negroes, as a minority, are dependent on their liberal-to-conservative allies, and that the one mistake Negroes must never make, whatever they say publicly, is to be genuinely independent in policy or action.)

One of the things that made Malcolm unique among the well-known figures of his time was his implacable opposition to this position, its assumptions and its consequences. He never tired of exposing and discrediting it. This approach disarms you, he told black people whenever and wherever he could; it blocks the organization of the masses on a proper basis; it makes Toms out of you, he said, using the strongest language he knew.

If someone said to Malcolm, "But Negroes are a minority, aren't they?" he would challenge a proposition that many people regard as self-evident. It all depends on where you stand and what you are looking at, he would insist. Whites, not blacks, are a minority in many Southern counties. And in Washington, D. C. And in Harlem. You say you're talking about something bigger than that, you're talking about the country, the nation? All right, but make sure you also talk about something bigger than the United States.

There are two schools of thought among American Negroes, he said at a meeting in New York on April 8, 1964, in the transition period. Of one school, he said,

> Their thinking is usually domestic, confined to the boundaries of America, and they always look upon themselves as a minority. When they look upon themselves upon the

American stage, the American stage is a white stage. So a black man standing on that stage in America automatically is in the minority. . . .

Whereas the other segment or section in America, known as the black nationalists . . . don't look upon themselves as Americans. They look upon themselves as a part of dark mankind. They see the whole struggle not within the confines of the American stage, but they look upon the struggle on the world stage. And, in the world context, they see that the dark man outnumbers the white man. On the world stage the white man is just a microscopic minority. [1]

These different ways of viewing the majority-minority question produce different attitudes, strategies and tactics. The Afro-American whose "scope is limited to the United States" feels

He is the underdog, and in his struggle he always uses an approach that is a begging, hat-in-hand, compromising approach.

But the Afro-American with the international outlook

uses a different approach in trying to struggle for his rights. He doesn't beg. He doesn't thank you for what you give him, because you are only giving him what he should have had a hundred years ago. He doesn't think you are doing him any favors. [2]

So the international approach is justified and should be cultivated, if only because of the superiority of its psychological results: Black people who think internationally, from a "majority" rather than a "minority" angle, tend to acquire higher morale, greater self-confidence, more militancy and tenacity — precisely the qualities that fighters for freedom need and that the communications and educational media discourage.*

---

* Political minorities can reap benefits from such an approach too. The editors of *Monthly Review*, an independent socialist magazine, have written: "Socialists in the United States, for example, have got to stop thinking of themselves as a tiny minority with the task – which many of them have already concluded is hopeless – of making a spe-

But Malcolm's internationalism did not rest solely on its psychological by-products. It was for him above all the source of allies for Afro-Americans. As he said to a rally of the Organization of Afro-American Unity on December 13, 1964:

> We need allies; and as long as you and I think that we can only get allies from the Bronx, or allies, you know, from up on the Grand Concourse, I mean where you don't live; as long as you and I think that's the only source or area from which we can get allies, our source of allies is limited. But when we realize how large this earth is, and how many different people there are on it, and how closely they resemble us, then when we turn to them for some sort of aid, or to form alliances, then we'll make a little faster progress. [4]

(The reference to "the Bronx" is to white liberals; the resemblance between Afro-Americans and many people in other parts of the world refers not only to their common non-whiteness but also to their common oppression and exploitation by white imperialists.)

The best and most numerous allies of American Negroes, in Malcolm's opinion, were to be found abroad, and that was where he placed his primary emphasis in his last year. He set out to convince black people in this country and Africans, Arabs, Asians and Latin Americans that they have common interests and a common enemy—"the international power structure." The enemy was no longer invincible, the colonial revolution could not be stopped, the tide was turning in the favor of the oppressed—he hammered away at these truths in order to combat pessimism and apathy and to encourage self-reliance and initiative. His plan to have the United States government indicted

_____

cifically American revolution. Instead, they must think of themselves as members of an immense international movement, capable of embracing the overwhelming majority of mankind, which has the revolutionary task of defeating and overthrowing international imperialism. Psychologically speaking, this involves going over from the minority to the majority and from the losing side to the winning side; it means escaping from the inevitable parochialism, isolationism, and sectarianism of an internally oriented Left; it means acquiring new perspectives and a new conception of strategy and tactics." [3]

in the United Nations for racism was only one aspect of a far-reaching strategy to "internationalize our struggle." The OAAU, he hoped, not only would unite black people in the United States but would be a nucleus for bringing about common action by non-whites throughout the Western Hemisphere.

While Malcolm's thinking about alliances began with non-Americans, colored and white, it also turned, in his last year, to the possibility of alliances with American whites. (The question of alliances with other American Negro groups is dealt with in the chapter on "Organization.") Malcolm's views on this possibility had not become hardened at the time of his death; they were still evolving, while he tried to think out other, more urgent problems, such as the consolidation of his own movement. He probably felt that he could afford to take his time with the alliance question because, in his view, there could not be any meaningful alliance until black militants had a strong organization of their own, able to stand on its own feet and speak for a significant number of people. He was not interested in the kinds of black-white alliance, formal and informal, that have existed in the past, where the black component was usually only a helpless appendage or captive, rather than a full-fledged partner.

As a Black Muslim, Malcolm preached against any alliance with whites. On November 10, 1963, in one of his last Black Muslim speeches, he told a meeting in Detroit where non-Muslim Negroes were in the majority,

> I know some of you all think that some of them [whites] aren't enemies. Time will tell. [5]

But he himself had begun to rethink the question before then. As he told the *Young Socialist* on January 18, 1965:

> When I was in the Black Muslim movement I spoke on many white campuses and black campuses. I knew back in 1961 and '62 that the younger generation was much different from the older, and that many students were more sincere in their analysis of the problem and their desire to see the problem solved. [6]

When Malcolm announced his new movement at a press conference on March 12, 1964, he said:

> Whites can help us, but they can't join us. There can be no black-white unity until there is first some black unity. There can be no workers' solidarity until there is first some racial solidarity. We cannot think of uniting with others, until we have first united among ourselves. [7]

This was not an assertion that black and white working class solidarity was unnecessary or impossible. On the contrary, it was an explanation of one of the conditions for the attainment of interracial workers solidarity on a stable and effective foundation. In this statement Malcolm neither advocated nor rejected.solidarity or alliances between white workers and black workers – what he was saying was that before such a thing could happen, the Negro people would first have to organize and unite themselves independently. *First* organize themselves in their own movement, *then* think of uniting or allying with others. The implication was that any interracial alliance that might be formed later would be one between *movements,* rather than between individuals (black) on one side and organizations (white or white-controlled) on the other; when and if an alliance then took place, Negroes would have their own movement inside it and would be better able to protect their interests inside the alliance than they could as individuals.

One week later, however, Malcolm expressed a somewhat different position. We have already quoted, in the previous chapter, from their March 19, 1964, interview A. B. Spellman's question whether Malcolm intended to collaborate with labor unions, socialists and other such groups and Malcolm's reply that his movement would work with anybody sincerely interested in eliminating injustices that Negroes suffer at the hands of Uncle Sam. Later in that interview the following exchange took place:

> Spellman: Can the race problem in America be solved under the existing political-economic system?
> Malcolm X: No.
> Spellman: Well then, what is the answer?
> Malcolm X: It answers itself.
> Spellman: Can there be any revolutionary change in

America while the hostility between black and white working classes exists? Can Negroes do it alone?

Malcolm X: Yes. They'll never do it with working class
whites. The history of America is that working class whites
have been just as much against not only working Negroes,
but *all* Negroes, period, because all Negroes are working
class within the caste system. The richest Negro is treated
like a working class Negro. There never has been any
good relationship between the working class Negro and the
working class whites. I just don't go along with – there
can be no worker solidarity until there's first some black
solidarity. There can be no white/black solidarity until
there's first some black solidarity. We have got to get our
problems solved first and then if there's anything left to
work on the white man's problems, good, but I think one
of the mistakes Negroes make is this worker solidarity
thing. There's no such thing – it didn't even work in Russia.
Right now it was supposedly solved in Russia but as soon
as they got their problems solved they fell out with China. [8]

Close examination shows that this March 19 statement
not only contradicts the March 12 statement – its parts contradict each other as well. Malcolm begins with undeniable
facts – the bad relations between white and black workers,
the historic hostility toward all Negroes. Now differing
conclusions can be reached from these facts: One possible
conclusion is that because these bad relations have existed
in the past, they will always exist in the future. Another
possible conclusion is that although they have existed in
the past, these bad relations can, under certain changed
conditions, be eliminated in the future. Malcolm clearly
leans to the first, but instead of expounding and defending
it, he suddenly, in his March 19 statement, switches back
to the March 12 theme that there can be no white-black
solidarity until there is first black solidarity. "First," however, implies "second." First black solidarity, second – what?
Then, immediately after voicing this implication that something about working class solidarity follows from the "first,"
Malcolm asserts that there is no such thing as working class
solidarity, it has never really worked. In fact, he now appears to be saying that working class solidarity is not
necessary anyhow – Negroes have to solve their own problems first and can do so without working class solidarity
or alliances.

How explain all of this? It may help to know that the
March 12 statement was very carefully formulated on paper
by Malcolm and his associates. They labored over it for
several days (and were quite bitter to see it ignored by
virtually the whole press – the sole exception being *The
Militant*). The section in the statement on solidarity represented something new for them – this was a problem they
had not had to bother with in the Nation of Islam – and
they gave it serious attention. And since it was a collective
position, it may also have been a compromise between
those who favored eventual working class solidarity and
those who regarded it as utopian or harmful.

Malcolm's interview with Spellman, on the other hand,
was unrehearsed. It may be that in answering Spellman's
question Malcolm at first reverted out of habit to the position he had long held as a Black Muslim; then, half-way
through, recalling the new position he had reached with his
associates in the Muslim Mosque, Inc., he introduced that
too; and finally, aware of the inconsistency between the
first two parts, he declared "there's no such thing" as
working class solidarity and never has been – so why
bother talking about it?

That is only speculation, however. What can safely be
said now, on the basis of the March 12 and March 19
statements, is that in the transition period, shortly after
the split, Malcolm held in his mind at the same time two
conflicting and unresolved views on black-white working
class relations – one which denied or belittled the possibility
or necessity of an alliance between them in the future, after
the Negroes had first united themselves; and another, which
left the question open, postponing a decision until after
black unification had taken place.

Then Malcolm went to Africa in the spring of 1964,
where he discussed this and related questions with people
he respected. On his return he said, during the question
period at a meeting on May 29, 1964:

> In my recent travels into the African countries and others,
> it was impressed upon me the importance of having a
> working unity among all peoples, black as well as white.
> But the only way this is going to be brought about is

that the black ones have to be in unity first. 9

The formulation is very revealing: The importance of having a working unity was "impressed upon" him. It was not reached at his own initiative — it was impressed upon him. But he does not deny or refute the idea itself, he offers no argument against it. All he has is a condition: "the black ones have to be in unity first." It is precisely the same condition he had set in the March 12 statement, and his position on the issue is substantially the same as the one he took then. He is not saying on May 29, as he did on March 19, that a working unity (or alliance) is not possible or necessary.

Later in the same meeting Malcolm was even more explicit:

> We will work with anyone, with any group, no matter what their color is, as long as they are genuinely interested in taking the type of steps necessary to bring an end to the injustices that black people in this country are afflicted by. No matter what their color is, no matter what their political, economic or social philosophy is, as long as their aims and objectives are in the direction of destroying the vulturous system that has been sucking the blood of black people in this country, they're all right with us. 10

This position Malcolm maintained to the end of his life. In the final period he only added to it. After his second trip to Africa, he discussed the relations between militant whites and militant blacks at a New York meeting on January 7, 1965:

> You have all types of people who are fed up with what's going on. You have whites who are fed up, you have blacks who are fed up. The whites who are fed up can't come uptown [to Harlem] too easily because people uptown are more fed up than anybody else, and they are so fed up it's not so easy to come uptown.
>
> Whereas the blacks uptown who come downtown usually are the type, you know, who almost lose their identity — they lose their soul, so to speak — so that they are not in a position to serve as a bridge between the militant whites

and the militant blacks; that type can't do it. I hate to hit him like that, but it's true. He has lost his identity, he has lost his feeling, and . . . he usually has lost his contact with Harlem himself. So that he serves no purpose, he's almost rootless, he's not uptown and he's not fully downtown.

So when the day comes when the whites who are *really* fed up – I don't mean these jive whites, who pose as liberals and who are not, but those who are fed up with what is going on – when *they* learn how to establish the proper type of communication with those uptown who are fed up, and they get some coordinated action going, you'll get some changes. You'll get some changes. And it will take both, it will take everything that you've got, it will take that. [11]

The meaning here is unmistakable: collaboration between militant whites and militant blacks, though difficult to bring about, is necessary ("it will take both") for the achievement of meaningful change.

Around this same time, in the last weeks of Malcolm's life, Marlene Nadle had been interviewing him and attending his meetings. She quotes his answer to a question asked by a black nationalist in Harlem, where Malcolm ended by saying:

"I'm not going to be in anybody's straitjacket. I don't care what a person looks like or where they come from. My mind is wide open to anybody who will help get the ape off our back."

The people that he feels can best help are the students, both black and white. But he considers all militant whites possible allies.

He qualifies the possibility. And woven into the qualifications are the threads of the emotions running through Harlem.

"If we are going to work together, the blacks must take the lead in their own fight. In phase one, the white led. We're going into phase two now."

"This phase will be full of rebellion and hostility. Blacks will fight whites for the right to make decisions that affect the struggle in order to arrive at their manhood and self-respect."

"The hostility is good," Malcolm said. "It's been bottled

up too long. When we stop always saying yes to Mr. Charlie and turning the hate against ourselves, we will begin to be free."

How did he plan to get white militants to work with him or even to walk into the Theresa with the kind of slings and arrows he was sending out?

There was the half-smile again. Then, thoughtfully stroking his new-grown beard, he said, "We'll have to try to rectify that."

He admitted that it would be difficult to get militant whites and blacks together. "The whites can't come uptown too easily because the people aren't too friendly. The black who goes downtown loses his identity, loses his soul. He's in no position to be a bridge because he has lost his contact with Harlem. Our Negro leaders have never had contact, so they can't do it.

"The only person who could is someone who is completely trusted by the black community. If I were to try, I would have to be very diplomatic, because there are parts of Harlem where you don't dare mention the idea."[12]

The idea could not be mentioned in parts of Harlem, but Malcolm was thinking about it. He had not yet committed himself to putting the idea into practice – other problems were too pressing – but he already was turning it over in his mind and discussing it out loud.

It is important to note that Malcolm, in these last two citations from January and February, 1965, was not discussing the class character of the white forces with whom militant blacks would probably collaborate: he was talking about "militant whites," not white workers. On the basis of his own experience and observation, he had come to believe, as Marxists believe, that Negroes need and will find dependable allies among certain whites. But, like most Americans who became radical in the 1950s and 1960s (when the labor movement remained in the grip of conservative or reactionary bureaucrats), he did not share the belief of the Marxists that the working class, including a decisive section of the white workers as well as of the black workers, will play a leading role in the alliance that will end both racism and capitalism.

Malcolm was pro-socialist in the last year of his life, but

not yet a Marxist. He saw the white workers only as they were (politically immature, lacking in independence, blinded by prejudice), and not as they might or would become under different conditions. He saw and said that the capitalist world was in crisis and certain to experience stormy change, but he did not see that the American workers would be swept up in that crisis and altered by it. He pointed out that American markets were being shrunk by the advance of the world revolution, and he called attention to the strides of automation, but he did not foresee that the crises created by these factors would compel the capitalists to launch a drive against the living standards of the American workers, and that this in turn would radicalize the presently conservative American workers, including their attitudes toward the Negroes, and drive them in self-interest toward collaboration with the Negro people against their common enemy.

Malcolm did not expect such changes, or at least had not yet fitted them into his picture of the future. But it is certain that if he had lived long enough to witness such changes, or even the beginning of such changes, he would have welcomed an alliance with radicalized white workers and their organizations. As he said at the end of the transition period, "We will work with anyone, with any group, no matter what their color is, as long as they are genuinely interested in taking the type of steps necessary to bring an end to the injustices that black people in this country are afflicted by." Once he had shaken himself free of Black Muslim dogma, the thing that counted with him in alliances was their nature and goal, not the color of the skin of those who participated in them.

V. SEPARATISM AND
BLACK NATIONALISM

Along with new moods and trends that appeared in the Negro community in the last decade of Malcolm's life, new words and expressions entered the American vocabulary, and old ones changed their meaning. An example is the word "integration," about which Malcolm said in the *Autobiography:*

> The word has no real meaning. I ask you: in the racial sense in which it's used so much today, whatever 'integration' is supposed to mean, can it precisely be defined? [1]

The trouble is not only that the word is not precisely defined, but that different groups use it to mean different things.

When some people speak of integration, they mean any action, court ruling or law that eliminates segregation or discrimination in one or more areas. They call it integration if one Negro is added to a police force or if five Negro children are admitted to a previously all-white school. Some in this group assert that integration already exists in the North, and that the task is to make the South like the North. Others hold that society is not yet integrated in the North, but that it will become integrated by the addition of separate acts of desegregation, one by one, over an indefinite period of time. Integration, thus defined, is condemned and rejected by many black people as tokenism and gradualism. It is not that they object to the desegregation of any one or more areas, but that they see this concept of integration as a trick or device for denying them genuine and complete freedom now or in the foreseeable future.

A second way in which integration is used is as "complete assimilation." James Farmer says that this, until recently, was what he and CORE meant by integration and sought to achieve (it is still the objective of the more conservative civil rights groups). Complete assimilation, says Farmer, is an ideal, of "ultimate goodness," under which there would be "a kind of random dispersal of Negroes throughout the society and the economy. There would be no Negro neighborhoods. . . . America would be a land of individuals who were American and nothing else." [2] But some Negroes, including most of those in CORE in 1966, have concluded that while this concept of integration may be fine as an ideal, it is too remote or impractical to serve present needs. Others are openly hostile to it. They don't want to be dispersed, because they have racial pride, because they prefer to live together, or because dispersal could be a method of dividing Negroes physically and reducing their ability to defend their common interests against whites, whose good intentions they have little reason to believe in.

There were and are other interpretations and definitions, but these are enough to explain why Malcolm did not accept integration as his goal.*

Another word used in several different ways is "separation." (This should not under any circumstances be confused with "segregation," a system that is *imposed* on blacks by whites; liberals often insist on equating the two.)

Sometimes separation refers to a tendency among black people in this country favoring their withdrawal into a nation of their own, either in Africa or in a portion of the territory that now makes up the United States. (In what follows the word "separatism" will be used, wherever possible, to denote this particular concept of separation.)

At other times separation is used as the opposite of assimilation (integration-as-complete-assimilation). Thus a black man may advocate separation to signify his hostility to being assimilated and his desire for the continued protection and warmth of the Negro community either in

---

* Integration is "irrelevant," said Stokely Carmichael in the spring of 1966, after he became chairman of the Student Nonviolent Coordinating Committee and was charged with taking it "down the Malcolm X road."

the America of today or in a future, desegregated, America. The emphasis here is on the voluntary preservation of a Negro community inside the United States as opposed to its disappearance, whereas "separatism" favors the withdrawal of Negroes into a nation outside or apart from the United States.

Separation is also used sometimes in a narrower – an organizational – sense. While certain Negro leaders insist that there must be integration in the organizations in the freedom movement, by which they mean that their composition must be interracial, some black people insist there must be separation in the freedom movement, by which they mean that all-black organizations must lead the movement and decide its policies. (It should be noted that the goals of an organization cannot be deduced merely from its racial composition. There have been and are all-black organizations whose goal is "integration." One of the best-known was A. Philip Randolph's Negro March on Washington Movement in the 1940s, which was formed on an all-black basis because that was believed to be the best way to recruit Negroes, although its objectives were the ending of discrimination and segregation in employment and the armed forces. It was for "separation" as an organizational form but against "separation" in every other sense.)

Malcolm was and remained in favor of maintaining and strengthening the Negro community, and he was and remained in favor of all-black organization in the struggle for freedom, but he changed his views on separatism in the last year of his life.

Another term requiring examination is the one that was most frequently applied to Malcolm after he left the Black Muslims – "black nationalism." Not much light on this subject can be gleaned from most of the press, white or Negro. As they employ it, black nationalism is little more than an epithet: "black supremacy," "racism in reverse," "the black counterpart of Ku Kluxism," etc.* All you can learn about

---

* During the Mississippi march to Jackson in June, 1966, SNCC chairman Stokely Carmichael "was repeatedly pressed with questions from TV and newspapers asking if he was a 'black nationalist'. . . 'Black nationalism in this country means "anti-white,"' Carmichael said. 'That's the trick they're trying to put me in.'" 3

black nationalism from this source is that you can't learn about black nationalism from this source.

It is also difficult, unfortunately, to get a clear picture of black nationalism as a tendency in the United States from many of the people and groups that consider themselves black nationalists. Although they share a common designation, they are divided over a definition and disagree, sometimes sharply, over important questions of policy and program. Some day this situation may change; some day the many small black nationalist groups may come together into a single strong organization or federation of organizations commanding the allegiance of most people who think of themselves as black nationalists; that is, some day black nationalism may become a movement rather than a tendency or group of tendencies. When that occurs, "black nationalism" will come to mean what that movement stands for, both among the masses and the professors who compile dictionaries.

Most academic attempts at a definition so far have created as many problems as they have solved. Instead of starting with a study of American black nationalists and their ideas and activities, and deriving their definition from that, they too often tend to start with a definition of nationalism *in general*, stick the word "black" in front of it, and think the work is done when it has hardly begun. One wonders how they would have proceeded if the tendency we are discussing had chosen or been given another name – say "black internationalism" (which would have been as appropriate as the name they now have). Where would we get in an analysis of the German Nazi movement, which called itself "National Socialism," if we began with a definition of socialism in general, then put the word national in front of that, etc.?

If we understand that the nature of a thing or tendency has primacy over the name given it, if we put the name in a subordinate position and do not let it distract or over-influence us, then black nationalism can be seen as approximately the following: It is the tendency for black people in the United States to unite as a group, as a people, into a movement of their own to fight for freedom, justice and equality. Animated by the desire of an oppressed minority to decide its own destiny, this tendency holds that black people must control their own movement and the political, economic and social institutions of the black community. Its characteristic attributes include racial pride, group consciousness, hatred of white supremacy, a striving for independence from white control, and identification with black and non-white oppressed groups in other parts of the world.

This was what James Farmer was talking about when he said that "black nationalism is the dominant mood of the Negro masses in the United States today."[4]   This was what C. Eric Lincoln was writing about in 1964 when he coined the term "mood ebony" to describe the sentiment growing among American Negroes, although he tried, rather unsuccessfully, to distinguish this "mood-ebony" from "black nationalism."[5]   And this was what was meant, earlier in this century, when people referred to someone as "a race man."

Understood in this light, it is plain that black nationalism in the United States today does have some of the features of "nationalism in general," or what the academicians call "classic" or "ideal" or "model" nationalism; and that it is similar in certain respects to the black nationalism found in Africa. But it also differs in at least one basic respect from both classic nationalism and African black nationalism. The thing that is unique about it is that, despite its name, it does not share (or does not yet share) a commitment to a struggle for a separate black nation (what we have above termed "separatism"). One can be both a black nationalist and a separatist, but one can also be a black nationalist without being a separatist.*

To grasp the full meaning of the evolution of Malcolm's thinking that is documented in this chapter, it helps to know

---

* How long this will be true no one can now foretell, but it is already possible to see the two directions in which the present situation can change: If racism is completely eliminated in the near future (and that will take a profoundly revolutionary reconstruction of the American economy, political structure and educational system), then the reasons for the existence of black nationalism will disappear, and it may fade away before becoming separatist. But if racism is not uprooted soon and if black people reach the conclusion that full equality is not attainable in the foreseeable future, separatist moods and activities are sure

that Malcolm began in 1964 to make this distinction between black nationalism and separatism.

As a Black Muslim leader, Malcolm preached separatism
with the same vigor that he did the rest of Muhammad's
doctrine. In his last public speech as a Black Muslim – on
December 1, 1963, when he made the "chickens come home
to roost" remark – he presented it as follows:

> The Honorable Elijah Muhammad teaches us that a de-
> segregated theater or lunch counter won't solve our prob-
> lems. Better jobs won't even solve our problems. An in-
> tegrated cup of coffee isn't sufficient pay for 400 years
> of slave labor, and a better job in the white man's factory
> or position in his business is, at best, only a temporary
> solution. The only lasting or permanent solution is com-
> plete separation on some land that we can call our own.
> The Honorable Elijah Muhammad teaches us that the
> race problem can easily be solved, just by sending these
> 22 million ex-slaves *back to our own homeland* where we
> can live in peace and harmony with our own kind. But
> this government should provide the transportation, plus
> everything else we need to get started again in our own
> country. This government should provide everything we
> need in machinery, materials and finance; enough to last
> us from 20 to 25 years, until we can become an inde-
> pendent people *in our own country.*
> If this white government is afraid to let her 22 million
> ex-slaves go back to our own country and to our own
> people, then America must set aside some separate terri-
> tory here in the Western Hemisphere, where the two races
> can live apart from each other, since we certainly don't
> get along peacefully while we are here together.
> The size of the territory can be judged according to our
> own population. If our people number one-seventh of
> America's total population, then give us one-seventh of
> this land. We don't want any land in the desert, but where
> there is rain and much mineral wealth.
> We want fertile, productive land on which we can farm

---

to grow among Negroes as a whole as well as among those who can
now be considered black nationalists. In that case, the historical judgment will be that black nationalism in its present phase was only
embryonic, incipient, not fully developed, and that its transformation
into separatism or classic nationalism was inevitable.

and provide our own people with sufficient food, clothing and shelter. This government must supply us with the machinery and other tools needed to dig into the earth. Give us everything we need for them from 20 to 25 years, until we can produce and supply our own needs.

If we are a part of America, then part of what she is worth belongs to us. We will take our share and depart, then this white country can have peace. *What is her net worth?* Give us our share in gold and silver and let us depart and go back to our own homeland in peace.

We want no integration with this wicked race that enslaved us. We want complete separation from this race of devils. But we should not be expected to go back to our own homeland *empty-handed.* After 400 years of slave-labor, we have some *"back-pay"* coming, a bill owed to us that must be collected.

If the government of white America truly repents of its sins against our people, *and atones by giving us our true share, only then can America save herself!*

But if America waits for Almighty God himself to step in and force her into a "just settlement," God will take this entire continent away from her; and she will cease to exist as a nation. . . .

White America, wake up and take heed, before it is too late! [6]

But what if white America would not wake up and take heed – would the "only" solution have to wait for Almighty God to step in? Malcolm's ability as a speaker enabled him to extract from the separatist theme all the emotional appeal it held for people resentful toward the tokenism that is called integration, but it could not conceal the fact that the Black Muslim method or program for achieving separatism was vague and indefinite, or the fact, which Malcolm was to acknowledge after the split, that "at no time did he [Muhammad] ever enter into any activity or action that was designed to bring any of this into existence." [7]

In his last months as a Black Muslim, Malcolm remained "orthodox" when speaking to the members of the Nation of Islam and assigned the main role in achieving separatism to Allah. But when he spoke to non-Muslim Negroes, as in his Detroit speech on November 10, 1963, he transferred the question from the religious sphere to the political.

Discussing "separation" and "black nationalism" and "revolution" as though they were all the same thing, he implied that Allah could use human help – revolutionary help:

> When you want a nation, that's called nationalism. When the white man became involved in a revolution in this country against England, what was it for? He wanted this land so he could set up another white nation. That's white nationalism. The French Revolution was white nationalism. The Russian Revolution – yes, it was – white nationalism. You don't think so? Why do you think Khrushchev and Mao can't get their heads together? White nationalism. All the revolutions that are going on in Asia and Africa today are based on what? – black nationalism. A revolutionary is a black nationalist. He wants a nation . . . If you're afraid of black nationalism, you're afraid of revolution. And if you love revolution, you love black nationalism.[8]

When the split came, Malcolm's position began to change. But the change was partial and gradual. At the March 12, 1964 press conference where he announced the formation of the Muslim Mosque, Inc., he said:

> I still believe that Mr. Muhammad's analysis of the problem is the most realistic, and that his solution is the best one. This means that I too believe the best solution is complete separation, with our people going back home, to our own African homeland.
>
> But separation back to Africa is still a long-range program, and while it is yet to materialize, 22 million of our people who are still here in America need better food, clothing, housing, education and jobs *right now.* . . .
>
> Our political philosophy will be black nationalism. Our economic and social philosophy will be black nationalism. Our cultural emphasis will be black nationalism. . . .
>
> The political philosophy of black nationalism means: we must control the politics and politicians of our community. They must no longer take orders from outside forces. We will organize, and sweep out of office all Negro politicians who are puppets for the outside forces. [9]

Thus Malcolm did not reject "complete separation" at the time of the split. He still embraced it, but now he put it in the category of a "long-range" program – an ultimate rather than an immediate objective. He did not call his new movement separatist; he gave it the designation of "black nationalist" to distinguish it from the Nation of Islam, which had never called itself that.

One week later, in his March 19 interview with A. B. Spellman, Malcolm interjected, when Spellman asked about his program for achieving "your goals of separation":

> A better word to use than separation is independence. This word separation is misused. The 13 colonies separated from England but they called it the Declaration of Independence; they don't call it the Declaration of Separation, they call it the Declaration of Independence. When you're independent of someone you can separate from them. If you can't separate from them it means you're not independent of them. [10]

But Spellman had only used the term used by Malcolm himself earlier in the interview:

> I believe that his [Muhammad's] analysis of the race problem is the best one and his solution is the only one. . . .
> The political philosophy of the Muslim Mosque will be black nationalism, the economic philosophy will be black nationalism, and the social philosophy will be black nationalism. And by political philosophy I mean we still believe in the Honorable Elijah Muhammad's solution as complete separation. The 22,000,000 so-called Negroes should be separated completely from America and should be permitted to go back home to our African homeland, which is a long-range program; so the short-range program is that we must eat while we're still here, we must have a place to sleep, we must have clothes to wear, we must have better jobs, we must have better education; so that although our long-range political philosophy is to migrate back to our African homeland, our short-range program must involve that which is necessary to enable us to live a better life while we are still here. We must be in complete control of the politics of the so-called Negro community; we must gain complete control over the politicians in the

so-called Negro community, so that no outsider will have any voice in the so-called Negro community. [11]

At this point—early in the transition period—there was still room in Malcolm's exposition of black nationalism for "separation" (back to Africa). But it was soon to drop out altogether, even as a long-range objective. On April 3, when he spoke at a CORE rally in Cleveland on "The Ballot or the Bullet," Malcolm began to explain black nationalism from a somewhat different angle:

> The political philosophy of black nationalism means that the black man should control the politics and the politicians in his own community; no more. The black man in the black community has to be re-educated into the science of politics so he will know what politics is supposed to bring him in return. . . . The political philosophy of black nationalism is being taught in the Christian church. It's being taught in the NAACP. It's being taught in CORE meetings. It's being taught in SNCC meetings. It's being taught in Muslim meetings. It's being taught where nothing but atheists and agnostics come together. It's being taught everywhere. [12]

If black nationalism meant "no more" than the Negro's control of his own community, of his own politics (and did not necessarily require a belief in separatism), then Malcolm was completely justified in seeing elements of black nationalism developing in organizations that were strongly opposed to back-to-Africa separatism. At any rate, his explanation of black nationalism in Cleveland did not contain even a mention of separation or separatism.

Five days later, Malcolm spoke on "The Black Revolution" at the Militant Labor Forum in New York. Like the Cleveland speech, it was a presentation and defense of the black nationalist outlook. At one point he said:

> All of our people have the same goals, the same objective. That objective is freedom, justice, equality. All of us want recognition and respect as human beings. We don't want to be integrationists. Nor do we want to be

separationists. We want to be human beings. Integration is only a method that is used by some groups to obtain freedom, justice, equality and respect as human beings. Separation is only a method that is used by other groups to obtain freedom, justice, equality or human dignity.

Our people have made the mistake of confusing the methods with the objectives. As long as we agree on objectives, we should never fall out with each other just because we believe in different methods or tactics or strategy to reach a common objective.

We have to keep in mind at all times that we are not fighting for integration, nor are we fighting for separation. We are fighting for recognition as human beings. We are fighting for the right to live as free humans in this society. 13

That was certainly a lot different from the March 12 and March 19 statements. Later in this New York meeting, during the discussion period, Malcolm was asked a question which gave him an opportunity to discuss the relation between black nationalism and separatism. The question, written out, referred to a statement in a pamphlet, *Freedom Now: A New Stage in the Struggle for Black Emancipation,* containing the Socialist Workers Party's 1963 convention resolution.[14] But Malcolm did not choose to use the question to expound his views on separatism. Instead, he said:

"A pamphlet, *Freedom Now,* is on sale in the back"–good plug–"and it contains the statement, 'All separatists are nationalists but not all nationalists are separatists.'" I don't know anything about that. "What is your view on this? Can one be a black nationalist even though not interested in a separate, independent black nation? Similarly, is every integrationist necessarily an assimilationist?" Well, as I said earlier, the black people I know don't want to be integrationists, nor do they want to be separationists – they want to be human beings. Some of them choose integration, thinking that this method will bring them respect as a human being, and others choose separation, thinking that that method or tactic will bring them respect as a human being. But they've had so much trouble attaining their objectives that they've gotten their methods mixed up with their objectives, and now, instead of calling themselves human beings, they're calling themselves integrationists and separationists, and they don't have either one – no. So I don't know about the integrationists and the assimilationists and the separationists, but I do know about the segregationists – that's the Americans. [15]

So there were three different positions expressed in the transition period. At first Malcolm reaffirmed his belief in separatism, then he implied that one could be a black nationalist without being a separatist, and then he showed a lack of interest in discussing separatism altogether.

On April 13, Malcolm left for Mecca and Africa, where he had discussions that led to big changes in his thinking on separatism and black nationalism. At a press conference held on the day of his return to New York, May 21, most of the questioning concerned Malcolm's revised views on race. But he was also asked if he still thought Negroes should return to Africa:

> Malcolm X replied that after speaking to African leaders he was convinced that "If black men become involved in a philosophical, cultural and psychological migration back to Africa, they will benefit greatly in this country."
> He compared this to the benefits he said Jews had derived from their identification with Israel. He went on to say that many African countries would welcome American Negroes, but that he thought Negroes should stay and fight in the U. S. for what was rightfully theirs. [16]

This remained Malcolm's position to the end. After his second trip to Africa, he told a HARYOU-ACT forum in Harlem on December 12, 1964, about the only kind of migration he favored:

> I believe this, that if we migrated back to Africa culturally, philosophically and psychologically, while remaining here physically, the spiritual bond that would develop between us and Africa through this cultural, philosophical and psychological migration, so-called migration, would enhance our position here, because we would have our contacts with them acting as roots or foundations behind us . . .
> And this is what I mean by a migration or going back to Africa – going back in the sense that we reach out to

them and they reach out to us. Our mutual understanding
and our mutual effort toward a mutual objective will bring
mutual benefits to the African as well as to the Afro-
American. [17]

To Pierre Berton's question on January 19, 1965–"But
you no longer believe in a black state?"–he gave the flat
answer:

> No, I believe in a society in which people can live like
> human beings on the basis of equality. [18]

And on January 24, when he read to an OAAU rally
the text of a telegram he had sent to George Lincoln Rock-
well, head of the American Nazi Party, he disassociated
himself not only from the abstentionism but also from the
separatism of the Nation of Islam:

> This is to warn you that I am no longer held in check
> from fighting white supremacists by Elijah Muhammad's
> separationist Black Muslim movement. . . . [19]

While Malcolm never publicly stated why he was changing
his position on separatism, it is clear that he stopped advocating it, even as a long-range position, by the end of
the transition period. What was not noticed at that time,
and was not discussed publicly for many months after that
by Malcolm or anyone else, was that he also began to
reconsider the whole question of black nationalism following his trip to Africa in the spring of 1964.

The first time Malcolm talked about this to any Americans outside of his associates in the OAAU was five weeks
before his death. On January 18, 1965, he gave an interview to representatives of the *Young Socialist*, and this
is how he answered their question, "How do you define
black nationalism, with which you have been identified?":

> I used to define black nationalism as the idea that the
> black man should control the economy of his community,
> the politics of his community, and so forth.
> But when I was in Africa in May, in Ghana, I was
> speaking with the Algerian ambassador who is extremely

militant and is a revolutionary in the true sense of the word (and has his credentials as such for having carried on a successful revolution against oppression in his country). When I told him that my political, social and economic philosophy was black nationalism, he asked me very frankly, well, where did that leave him? Because he was white. He was an African, but he was Algerian, and to all appearances he was a white man. And he said if I define my objective as the victory of black nationalism, where does that leave him? Where does that leave revolutionaries in Morocco, Egypt, Iraq, Mauritania? So he showed me where I was alienating people who were true revolutionaries, dedicated to overthrowing the system of exploitation that exists on this earth by any means necessary.*

So, I had to do a lot of thinking and reappraising of my definition of black nationalism. Can we sum up the solution to the problems confronting our people as black nationalism? And if you noticed, I haven't been using the expression for several months. But I still would be hard pressed to give a specific definition of the over-all philosophy which I think is necessary for the liberation of the black people in this country. 20

Actually, Malcolm had not altogether abandoned the expression "black nationalism." He had virtually stopped calling himself and the OAAU black nationalist. But since everyone else continued to call them by that label, and since he did not yet have an alternative label, he would accept its continued use in discussion and debate. Thus, for example, in his first reference to the OAAU in a radio panel discussion over Station WINS on February 18, 1965, he

---

* On returning from his first African trip, Malcolm wrote that the Algerian ambassador "had a razor-sharp mind, and was well-versed in the principles of revolution. His image of militant sincerity is still strongly pictured in my mind." ("We Are All Blood Brothers," *Liberator,* July, 1964) The author, after being informed by the Algerian mission to the United Nations that the Algerian ambassador to Ghana in May, 1964, was Mr. Taher Kaid, wrote to him, both at the Algerian Embassy in Accra and at the Algerian Ministry of Foreign Affairs in Algiers, asking him if he could supply information for this book about his discussions with Malcolm. Unfortunately, these letters were not sent until after the Ben Bella regime had been overthrown in Algeria and the Nkrumah regime had been overthrown in Ghana. This may explain why no reply was received.

carefully stated that it "is considered nationalist." No one on the panel paid the slightest attention to this formulation but kept on calling Malcolm and his movement black nationalist; in the subsequent exchanges Malcolm did the same, instead of continuing to make the distinction.

It was not until after the publication of the *Young Socialist* interview a few days after Malcolm's death that anyone looked back to see when Malcolm had stopped calling himself a black nationalist. It was at the end of May, right after his first trip abroad in 1964.

On his return from that trip, Malcolm spent the whole month of June organizing the OAAU in New York. When he had formed the Muslim Mosque, Inc., in March, he had said it was black nationalist. He did not say this about the OAAU at its first meeting on June 28, 1964. Nor did the "Statement of Basic Aims and Objectives of the Organization of Afro-American Unity," which he made public at that meeting, make any reference whatever to black nationalism. (See Appendix A for full text.)

Early in 1965, Malcolm announced that the OAAU was preparing a new program. It was to be presented in printed form by the OAAU at an Audubon rally on February 15, 1965. But Malcolm's home was bombed on February 14 and the February 15 rally was devoted to discussion mainly of that event. Presentation of the new "Basic Unity Program," dated February 15, was postponed to a subsequent meeting, and Malcolm was assassinated at the next meeting. But the "Basic Unity Program" did not call the OAAU black nationalist; it never even mentioned the expression. (See Appendix B for full text.)

Is it correct to still speak of Malcolm as a black nationalist when we know that he had stopped calling himself that and was questioning the adequacy of black nationalism as "the solution to the problems confronting our people"? The answer is yes, if we continue to use the definition of black nationalism attempted earlier in this chapter.

Malcolm became a black nationalist while he was in prison in the late 1940s – it was the starting point for all his thinking, the source of his strength and dynamism. And he remained a black nationalist to his last hour, however uncertain he became about what to call himself or the program that he was trying to formulate.

The most urgent need of the Negro people is their mobilization and unification into an independent movement to fight for their freedom. Black nationalism contributes to that process, in much the way that class consciousness contributes to the formation of an independent movement of workers for their emancipation from exploitation.

But black nationalism is a means, not the end; it is a means, but not the only means; it is probably an indispensable means toward the solution, but it is not the solution itself. It helps to build an independent movement, but it does not by itself provide the program that will lead such a movement to victory – any more than class consciousness by itself supplies all the answers for the workers.

Light can be shed on Malcolm's reappraisal if we understand that there is more than one variety of black nationalist. Relevant to this discussion is the variety that can be called pure-and-simple. (This was first discussed in a 1964 series of articles, later published under the title, *Marxism and the Negro Struggle.*[21])

The pure-and-simple black nationalist is concerned exclusively or primarily with the internal problems of the Negro community, with organizing it, with helping it to gain control of the community's politics, economy, etc. He is not concerned, or is less concerned, with the problems of the total American society, or with the nature of the larger society within which the Negro community exists. He has no theory or program for changing that society; for him that is the white man's problem.

At a New York symposium sponsored by the Committee to Aid the Monroe Defendants on May 1, 1962, Malcolm, after speaking on police brutality against blacks, was asked from the audience to comment on the fact that police were also brutal to whites. He said:

> As black people, against whom atrocity and brutality has been practiced in this country since we first landed here – by the whites – we're not interested in the hell that whites catch from whites. We're interested in solving our problems first. That's your problem – we're not interested in it. [22]

That was the reply of a pure-and-simple black nationalist. We have already quoted Malcolm's statement to A. B. Spellman early in the transition period: "We have got to get our problems solved first and then if there's anything left to work on the white man's problems, good . . ." That too was typical pure-and-simple black nationalism.

But while Malcolm was that kind of black nationalist in the transition period, he did not remain that kind. As he held discussions with people in Africa, in the Middle East, at the United Nations and in the United States, as he studied and thought and learned, he moved beyond pure-and-simple black nationalism — toward black nationalism plus. Plus what? "Radicalism," the third chapter of this book, has already shown from Malcolm's speeches and interviews that he was coming to the conclusion that radical changes have to be made in the society as a whole if black people are to achieve their freedom. This did not contradict his belief that blacks should control their own community; it was an addition to that belief.

The solution cannot be "summed up" as black nationalism. That means black nationalism plus fundamental social change, plus the transformation of the whole society. Malcolm still was looking for the name, but he was becoming black nationalist plus revolutionary. (We know he had great respect for the latter term; he may have hesitated to apply it to himself out of modesty, or because he thought it would be an added handicap in this country.)

What he was questioning about black nationalism was not its essence but its pure-and-simple form. He was questioning this because it "was alienating people who were true revolutionaries" — in this case, white revolutionaries. A pure-and-simple black nationalist wouldn't care what effect he had on whites, revolutionary or not. Malcolm cared because he intended to work with white revolutionaries; he knew their collaboration was needed if society was to be transformed.

Malcolm was beginning to think about the need to replace capitalism with socialism if racism was to be eliminated. He was not sure if it could be done, and he was not sure how it could be done, but he was beginning to believe that that was the road to be traveled.

His uncertainty about the right name to call himself arose from the fact that he was doing something new in the United States – he was on the way to a synthesis of black nationalism and socialism that would be fitting for the American scene and acceptable to the masses in the black ghetto. (An example of the tendency of revolutionary nationalism to grow over into and become merged with socialism can be seen in Cuba, where Castro and his movement began as nationalist.) Malcolm did not complete this synthesis before he was assassinated. It remains for others to complete what he began.

VI. ORGANIZATION

Because the tapes or transcriptions of many of Malcolm's 1964-65 speeches and interviews in the United States are available, it is relatively easy to follow, and judge, the evolution of his thinking on social and political questions. But it is difficult to assess his views on organization and how he dealt with the tasks of creating a new movement, because he did not discuss these questions in public. A dozen or two people, who worked with him in the leadership of the Muslim Mosque, Inc., and the Organization of Afro-American Unity, know about the practical organizational problems he faced and the ideas he had about solving them; for various reasons they have not discussed or written about these questions publicly. It is only fair to warn the reader that the present chapter is not based on any "inside" knowledge; that it touches, at most, on a few general aspects of things that were known or could be deduced by people not belonging to either of the two organizations headed by Malcolm.

The critics of Malcolm make much of the fact that his movement was small in numbers. James Farmer writes:

> After leaving the Muslims, Malcolm mostly talked. He had no program and no stomach for organizing a really effective organization (the Organization of Afro-American Unity could not have numbered more than 250 at the time of his death). [1]

It is doubtful that Farmer would apply similar if-you're-so-smart,-why-aren't-you-rich? criteria to himself and CORE. Didn't Farmer too "mostly talk" when CORE was first organized? Isn't "talk" (education, propaganda) a necessary means for attracting recruits to a new movement?

The OAAU was only eight months old when Malcolm was killed – if it had no more than 250 members then, did CORE have more than that when it was eight months old? Or even when it was eight years old? Wasn't it much harder to recruit to the OAAU than to CORE because of its different character? Isn't it presumptuous of Farmer to charge Malcolm with having "no stomach for organizing a really effective organization" when Malcolm was trying to organize not just another group seeking reforms, but an effective *revolutionary* movement – which, as he well knew, made him a marked man?

The task Malcolm set for himself in March, 1964, was truly formidable. Almost alone, surrounded by new as well as old enemies, he set out, on unfamiliar terrain, to build a movement that would challenge the most powerful government in the world. Farmer can sneer about his alleged ineffectiveness, but that government and its police agencies took Malcolm seriously. They regarded him as a danger, not just a talker, and they sighed with relief when he was killed.

Attorney Milton Henry, a friend of Malcolm from Pontiac, Michigan, tells of a discussion they had in a New York hotel room after an OAAU meeting on December 20, 1964. "Malcolm stretched his length full out on the sofa, leaned his head back, closed his eyes. He seemed terribly tired and worn. Exhausted. Used up." He told Henry he expected to be killed, and discussed some of the problems facing his movement: "There was so much to do and not really enough help doing it. He was in essence an evangelist – not an organizer. He deplored this, yet said that he knew so many black persons looked to him to be able to organize the entire black nationalist movement. It was a task of frightening dimensions. It was for one man an awful responsibility. But Malcolm had resigned himself and family to their expenditure upon just that project." [2]

"Not an organizer" – is that a correct appraisal? The record of his 12 years in the Nation of Islam shows that he was a brilliant, inventive, tireless and successful organizer. It would be more accurate to say that he was not primarily an organizer; that his talents as teacher and inspirer were greater than those as organizer.

Of course there were differences between being an organizer for Muhammad and organizing his own movement. In the first case, he accepted a doctrine and spent all his time promoting it; in the second case, he had to divide his time – to work out the philosophy and program of his movement as well as organize. In the first case, the structure of the organization was already set, the rules, framework and methods of operation already in existence; there already was an apparatus to be used or modified. In the second, he had to begin almost from scratch. He could not simply continue using former methods – he had to devise new ones, because he was not trying to create another Nation of Islam, with himself in place of Muhammad. He was trying to create a different kind of movement.

The Black Muslim organization was built around a mystique of leadership, demanding faith in and submission to a divine, all-wise chief. Malcolm rejected such a role for himself: "I do not pretend to be a divine man . . . nor am I an expert in any field," he said at the March 12, 1964, press conference after the split. The organization he had in mind would not only intervene in the freedom struggle from which the Black Muslims abstained – it would also be more democratic. Having seen how harmful its effects could be, he did not want another organization with a one-man leadership. He wanted a collective leadership, and although he saw the need for a disciplined and centralized organization, he wanted a different relationship between leaders and members than the Black Muslims had. He invited and welcomed criticism as well as advice and suggestions from members and non-members. He publicly disclaimed the right to speak for the OAAU on any question until the organization had decided where it stood. He wanted the members to be well-informed and independent-minded, rather than obedient handraisers. A constant admonition during his last year was: "Learn how to see for yourself and listen for yourself and think for yourself."

It was harder, much harder, to start and build that kind of movement than to recruit to the Nation of Islam (or CORE). Those who have built that kind of movement into a mass force in eight months are the only ones entitled to belittle Malcolm's organizational accomplishments.

James Farmer writes:

> A year before his assassination on February 21, 1965 –
> the first day of Brotherhood Week – Malcolm broke with
> the Muslims to found the Organization of Afro-American
> Unity, the very name of which indicates his desire to bring
> all Negroes – separationists and integrationists, Muslims,
> Christians, and others – under a single nationalist tent. [3]

This sloppiness about easily-checked facts is typical of
much of the writing about Malcolm. It is not true that he
started the OAAU when he left the Black Muslims – his
thinking had not gone that far, unfortunately. Instead, at
his March 12, 1964, press conference, he announced:

> I am going to organize and head a new mosque in New
> York City, known as the Muslim Mosque, Inc. This gives
> us a religious base, and the spiritual force necessary to
> rid our people of the vices that destroy the moral fiber
> of our community. . . . Our . . . philosophy will be black
> nationalism. . . . Many of our people aren't religiously
> inclined, so the Muslim Mosque, Inc., will be organized in
> such manner to provide for the active participation of all
> Negroes in our political, economic, and social programs,
> despite their religious or non-religious beliefs. [4]

Malcolm founded a religious organization first, because
he and most of the people willing to work with him at that
point wanted to remain Muslims although outside of the
Nation of Islam. But why found a religious organization
if its philosophy was to be secular – the spread of black
nationalism? There was a contradiction here, and a source
of confusion. Malcolm promised that the new mosque
would be so organized as to provide for participation of
"all Negroes" in the non-religious activities of his religious
organization. But how could that be? The very name of
the organization was an obstacle to the participation of
people who were not interested in Islam or were hostile
to it.

Speaking in Cleveland a few weeks later, on April 3,
Malcolm tried to explain:

> I would like to say, in closing, a few things concerning
> the Muslim Mosque, Inc., which we established recently in

New York City. It's true we're Muslims and our religion
is Islam, but we don't mix our religion with our politics
and our economics and our social and civil activities –
not any more. We keep our religion in our mosque. After
our religious services are over, then as Muslims we become
involved in political action, economic action and social
and civic action. We become involved with anybody, anywhere, any time and in any manner that's designed to
eliminate the evils, the political, economic and social evils
that are afflicting the people of our community. [5]

The change was clear – Malcolm's organization, unlike
the Black Muslims, *wanted* to work with non-Muslims. But
Malcolm's organization itself was Muslim. People who were
not Muslims and did not want to become Muslims, but who
did want to join Malcolm in the fight for freedom, were not
offered any organization to belong to. This was a serious
tactical mistake. Malcolm corrected it three months later,
but valuable time was lost during the period when interest
in his new course was at its height. Many more people
could have been recruited in those months if Malcolm's
organizational concepts had been fully worked out at the
time of the split, or if he had been able to complete his
break with religious sectarianism all at once.

Malcolm wanted to build a new nation-wide movement.
How did the formation of the Muslim Mosque, Inc., relate
to that perspective? At the end of March he told Carlos
Russell:

First we will continue to spread the philosophy of black
nationalism, then in the June convention where all of the
black nationalists of this country will meet, we will sit
down in seminars, and formulate the best approach towards
this end. It will not be unilateral; I mean by this that I will
not dictate, but rather it will come from the convention. [6]

So the Muslim Mosque, Inc., was not conceived as *the*
black nationalist organization, but as one of many which
would meet in convention and try to unite around a collectively agreed on approach and program. This may have
been one reason why Malcolm was not too concerned at
first about the inability of non-Muslim supporters to join
his mosque; he probably thought that they would be able

to get together organizationally in the non-religious movement that would emerge out of the June convention. (In the
end, the convention was not held, even though he postponed its date to August.)

Malcolm was very much concerned at this time about
avoiding even the appearance of sectarianism. To promote
the widest possible black unity, he sought the good will
and cooperation of the moderate Negro leaders and tried
to convince them he was not interested in "raiding" their
organizations. In his Cleveland CORE speech on April 3,
he said that the political philosophy of black nationalism
(which he defined without any mention of "separation")was
being taught in the Christian churches, the NAACP, CORE,
SNCC — "It's being taught everywhere." But how could unity
be achieved and divisions avoided?

> I have watched how Billy Graham comes into a city,
> spreading what he calls the gospel of Christ, which is only
> white nationalism. That's what he is – Billy Graham is a
> white nationalist; I'm a black nationalist. But since it's
> the natural tendency for leaders to be jealous and look
> upon a powerful figure like Graham with suspicion and
> envy, how is it possible for him to come into a city and
> get all the cooperation of the church leaders? . . .
> Billy Graham comes in preaching the gospel of Christ,
> he evangelizes the gospel, he stirs everybody up, but he
> never tries to start a church. If he came in trying to start
> a church, all the churches would be against him. So, he
> comes in talking about Christ and tells everybody who
> gets Christ to go to any church where Christ is; and in
> this way the churches cooperate with him. So we're going
> to take a page from his book.
> Our gospel is black nationalism. We're not trying to
> threaten the existence of any organization, but we're spread-
> ing the gospel of black nationalism. Anywhere there's a
> church that is also preaching and practicing the gospel of
> black nationalism, join that church. If the NAACP is
> preaching and practicing the gospel of black nationalism,
> join the NAACP. If CORE is spreading and practicing the
> gospel of black nationalism, join CORE. Join any organi-
> zation that has a gospel for the uplift of the black man.
> And when you get into it and see them pussyfooting or
> compromising, pull out of it because that's not black
> nationalism. We'll find another one.

> And in this manner the organizations will increase in number and in quantity and in quality, and by August, it is then our intention to have a black nationalist convention which will consist of delegates from all over the country who are interested in the political, economic and social philosophy of black nationalism. After these delegates convene, we will hold a seminar, we will hold discussions, we will listen to everyone. We want to hear new ideas and new solutions and new answers. And at that time, if we see fit to form a black nationalist party, we'll form a black nationalist party. If it's necessary to form a black nationalist army, we'll form a black nationalist army. [7]

But the analogy with Billy Graham was badly flawed. Graham could hope to get the cooperation of local churches because he was not trying to establish a church of his own, either on a city-wide or a nation-wide level. But Malcolm wanted, and openly said he wanted, to create a nation-wide movement, party or army at the proposed August convention. Was it realistic to expect the cooperation of Christian, NAACP, and similar leaders when they knew his aim was a new national movement whose aims would conflict with theirs? Malcolm correctly saw elements of black nationalism developing inside these moderate organizations; but when he urged people who agreed with him to join these organizations, did he really expect them to become leaders, and to be elected as delegates by these organizations, *between April and August*? If not, then what was the connection between his advice that they join such organizations and his remarks about the August convention? The organizational perspective in the transition period was certainly not clear.

The two things that Malcolm wanted simultaneously – to promote a new militant movement that would attract the best elements in the moderate organizations, and to avoid a head-on clash with the leaders of those organizations (or even win their cooperation!) – were simply not compatible. The last thing in the world the moderate leaders wanted was to be confronted by a national Malcolm-type movement. Malcolm at first bent over backwards because he did not want to antagonize or provoke them and because he wanted to show his sincerity about black unity. But he realized later that bending over backwards is not the proper stance for reaching the masses.

On April 13 Malcolm left for Mecca and Africa. While he was there, he became convinced that the Muslim Mosque, Inc., was not the proper vehicle for the non-religious activities he wanted to engage in. In May he helped to organize a group of black Americans living in an African country; the name they chose was the Organization of Afro-American Unity. Soon after he returned to New York at the end of May he decided that the black nationalist convention projected for August was not feasible, or would not be successful if held. So he set to work in June to build a new organization.

On June 24 he made public a letter which had been sent to "local and national heads of civil and human rights organizations and also to representatives of African nations currently in the United States." The letter said in part:

> A cross section of the Harlem community has been working for some time on the formation of an organization that would transcend all superficial, man made divisions between the Afro-American people of this country who are working for human rights, and that would in no way compete with already existing successful organizations.
>
> I have been requested, and indeed it is my pleasure, to announce the existence of the Organization of Afro-American Unity (OAAU), patterned after the letter and the spirit of the Organization of African Unity (OAU). Its purpose is to unite Afro-Americans and their organizations around a non-religious and non-sectarian constructive purpose for human rights.
>
> The Organization of Afro-American Unity is well aware of your interest, work, and involvement in freedom struggles over the years, and you have proven to be sincere in your area of endeavor.
>
> Therefore, the Organization of Afro-American Unity would like you to be its guest at a rally Sunday, June 28, 1964, at 8:00 p.m. at the Audubon Ballroom, 166th Street and Broadway in New York City, at which time the Organization of Afro-American Unity and its aims and objectives will be announced publicly. . . .

Malcolm was still bending over backwards. If he expected to involve these "local and national heads" in the OAAU by promising it would not "compete with already existing successful organizations" and by praising their sincerity, he was being naive. Perhaps he was not expecting it, and the invitation for collaboration may have been a move to put the onus for continued disunity on them. In any case, few of them attended the June 28 rally, and only a couple joined the organization.

At the rally Malcolm read aloud, explained and expanded on the OAAU's "Statement of Basic Aims and Objectives" (see Appendix A), membership applications were taken and the new organization was launched, with Malcolm as chairman. This was exactly 34 weeks before his assassination. He went abroad early in July, not returning until November 24, and he later spent two weeks in England (one in December, the other in February, 1965). So Malcolm was in the United States for only 12 of the 34 weeks between the foundation of the OAAU and his death.

The June "Statement of Basic Aims and Objectives" was evidently not considered sufficient. On January 17, 1965, Malcolm announced that an OAAU committee was working on a program. Early in February he stated that the program, which was "designed to galvanize the black masses of Harlem to become the instruments of their own liberation" and offered the only "alternative to violence and bloodshed," would be presented at an OAAU rally on February 15. This document, which Malcolm approved and accepted although he did not write it, was entitled the "Basic Unity Program" (see Appendix B). But Malcolm's home was bombed on February 14, and the February 15 meeting revolved around a discussion of that event, with presentation of the program postponed to the next meeting, February 21. That was the meeting where Malcolm was shot down, before he could speak about the program or anything else.

With only such meager information to go by, it is obvious that an adequate study of Malcolm's organizational conceptions is not yet possible. Until one or more of his close collaborators in 1964-5 tells the story of Malcolm's two organizations as it was experienced and understood from the inside, the most that can be added are some speculations.

When Malcolm assured the moderate Negro leaders in June that the OAAU would not compete with their organizations, he was not just being diplomatic; there is evidence that he did think of the OAAU in that way at that time. But how could he? What would be the OAAU's reason for existence if it did not provide a program of action, a method of operating and a perspective different from, and therefore opposed to, those of the other organizations in the field?

The answer, which cannot be given with certainty, is probably related to his views on black unity. He wanted to avoid all appearances of "factionalism." This was encouraged by certain African leaders. SNCC spokesmen John Lewis and Donald Harris, who ran into Malcolm in a hotel in Nairobi, Kenya, in the fall of 1964, where they had long talks with him as he was completing the final leg of his second African tour, reported that he told them the African leaders were willing to help the American freedom movement, "but they will not tolerate factionalism or support particular groups or organizations within the movement as a whole. It was with this in mind that he formed his Organization of Afro-American Unity." [8] Malcolm's "non-competitive" concept of the OAAU may have derived from his desire to win African support for his plan to get the United States government indicted in the United Nations.

Broadly speaking, and schematizing a little, there were two ways in which Malcolm could proceed in his quest for black unity. One was by negotiation, the other by struggle – and each implied a different kind of organization.

The first way was for Malcolm to form an organization whose main function would be to approach the existing organizations, reason with them and negotiate with them to obtain joint action. Its emphasis would be on points of agreement, not of disagreement. Given the moderate and liberal character of most of these groups, the chances of getting their agreement would be greater if Malcolm's organization were "not too militant" and its program "not too radical." Such an organization would tend to be loose rather than highly disciplined, it would not place heavy demands on its members, and it probably would not see any special or unique role for itself within the movement once the objective of black unity had been achieved.

The second way would require building an organization distinctly different from the moderate groups, with emphasis on those parts of its program that were different from theirs. It not only would be more radical than the others, but would have to compete with them for mass support, both among the people not affiliated with any organization and the ranks of the existing organizations. Using flexible tactics, it would seek to achieve united action by placing the leaders of the other organizations in a position where they would be forced to go along or face the prospect of being deposed or deserted by their followers. In such an organization the leaders and members would be animated by the conviction that freedom could be won only through *their* program and methods; internal education, external propaganda and the development of a strong sense of commitment would receive special attention.

The second way was undoubtedly harder and would take longer. But was there another and easier way that would result in what Malcolm wanted?

Malcolm was not sure at the beginning. In the transition period and even later, he seemed to be attracted by the first approach, or certain aspects of it. He could not fully embrace it because of the serious obstacles – he would not agree, as a price for unity, to abandon the advocacy of self-defense; he would not compromise on the need for genuine and complete independence from the white liberals and their politics; he would never accept Washington's foreign policy. Later, he appeared to be wavering between the two approaches and wondering if somehow they could be combined. Near the end, he was apparently moving in the direction of the second.

Around a month before his death, Malcolm discussed with Marlene Nadle self-defense and other differences with the moderate Negro leaders that impeded "the unity that he feels is one of the keys to the struggle." He said:

> It's not that there is no desire for unity, or that it is impossible, or that they might not agree with me behind closed doors. It's because most of the organizations are dependent on white money and they are afraid to lose it.

> I spent almost a year not attacking them, saying let's
> get together, let's do something. But they're too scared.
> I guess I will have to go to the people first and let the
> leaders fall in behind them. [9]

"To go to the people first and let the leaders fall in behind them" could not be done with a "non-competitive"
organization. However, Malcolm added, going to the people first did not mean that he ruled out cooperation with
the other leaders: he would still stress the areas and activities where the different groups could work together. "If we
are going into the ring," he said, "our right fist does not
have to become our left fist, but we must use a common
head if we are going to win." The words "I guess" signified
that Malcolm still was not completely certain, but the rest
of the statement indicated that at the end Malcolm's conception of his organization was changing from that of a
unity-broker toward that of the left fist of the freedom struggle. The final resolution of this problem was halted by the
assassins' bullets.

VII. MALCOLM AND HIS CRITICS

Malcolm was one of the most slandered and most misunderstood Americans of our time. Neither the slander nor the misunderstanding diminished after he left the Black Muslims; even the form they took remained essentially the same—that he was a racist and an advocate of violence. The truth is that he was an opponent of racism (which holds that one or some races are "superior" and ought to rule the others) who wanted to use the conditions created by racism, including the racial consciousness it fosters among its black victims, to bring about its abolition; and that what he advocated was self-defense by black people against the violence and terrorism used to keep them in a subordinate position. Most of the distortion on these two points is so crude that almost anyone who reads what Malcolm actually said can see through it.*

Not all the authors of anti-Malcolm statements are crude, however; some even make a claim to be objective. An example is Bayard Rustin, who is too smart to call Malcolm a racist. Rustin has had considerable prestige in sections of the civil rights, pacifist and radical movements (although

---

* This evidently does not apply to intellectuals like Irving Howe, who refuses to see any distinction between advocating self-defense and advocating violence, and persists in saying that Malcolm "talked violence." [1] James Farmer recognizes the distinction, but he too is reprehensible when, after explaining what Malcolm meant by self-defense, he tacks on the statement, "The danger in Malcolm's doctrine is that it may readily be subverted into an excuse for generalized and indiscriminate violence, generalized and indiscriminate revenge. A War: White vs. Black. I think Malcolm often succumbed to this danger, at least verbally. . . ." [2] The latter charge is absolutely unfounded; Malcolm foresaw the possibility of indiscriminate violence, and explained why it might occur if racist violence and oppression were not ended, and sometimes predicted that it would occur, but he never advocated it. Anyhow, since when should a doctrine be declared dangerous because it may be "subverted"?

it has been tarnished among militants in recent years by his efforts to get the Mississippi Freedom Democratic Party to accept Johnson's rotten compromise at the Atlantic City convention of the Democratic Party in August, 1964; his redbaiting of Students for a Democratic Society's march on Washington against the war in Vietnam in April, 1965, etc.); and many of his supporters consider him the best theorist and organizer of the freedom movement and the most qualified spokesman against the course that Malcolm represented. Hence the three articles he wrote in 1965 after Malcolm's death*—the most ambitious attempt yet made to evaluate Malcolm from a quasi-radical, left-liberal standpoint—are worth some attention.

"Now that he is dead," Rustin says, "we must resist the temptation to idealize Malcolm X, to elevate charisma to greatness."(2) The sentiment is pious, but misplaced. The only temptation Rustin faces is to disparage Malcolm, and he doesn't resist it hard. "Malcolm," he insists, "is not a hero of the movement, he is a tragic victim of the ghetto." (1) "For all of his militance, Malcolm was in many respects a conservative force in the Negro community. His violent rhetoric was a 'cop-out.'"(2) After Malcolm left the Black Muslims, "it was unclear whether he was running away from or toward something" (although two paragraphs later Rustin sees nothing unclear about Malcolm's direction: "Malcolm was moving toward the mainstream of the civil rights movement when his life was cut short"). (3) Rustin cannot even restrain himself from speaking

* The first appeared in the February 28 issue of the Socialist Party publication, *New America*, under the title "On Malcolm X." The second, with Tom Kahn as co-author, appeared in the same paper on March 24, under the title "The Mark of Oppression," and was also printed, with slight revisions, in another social-democratic publication, *Dissent*, Spring, 1965, under the title "The Ambiguous Legacy of Malcolm X." The third, a review of Malcolm's autobiography, appeared November 14 in *Book Week*, under the title "Making His Mark." Quotations from them will be indicated by (1), (2) and (3). While there are certain inconsistencies among the three articles, the third being less spiteful than the others, the approach in them is generally the same, and it is fair to examine them collectively. The second article was effectively answered by Robert Vernon in the May 24 and May 31, 1965 issues of *The Militant*, reprinted in this book as Appendix C.

about Malcolm's allegedly "anti-Semitic comments," although he knows very well that these comments were directed against dishonest shopkeepers, landlords and liberals, not against the Jewish people as a whole, or their religion.

Rustin pays tribute to Malcolm's personal qualities, especially in the third article, but since the liberal-led, nonviolent, gradualist "civil rights movement" is the only thing that is meaningful to Rustin, the highest praise he can think of is that "Malcolm was a help to the established civil rights organizations, because he frightened white people into negotiating with Dr. King and James Farmer."(1) Later even this praise is partially taken back: "But whom did Malcolm really frighten? Surely not Goldwater or Eastland or the racist power structure. Malcolm frightened and worried white liberals, those most in sympathy with the movement, and those with guilt feelings. But while all these groups began perceiving the need for a more fundamental movement that would encompass and activate broader sections of the Negro community, many hostile or indifferent whites were let off the hook. It was a relief to know that extremism existed on both sides. A moderate position became tenable." (2) So Malcolm gets blamed for the hostility and indifference of whites who did not support the civil rights movement! Rustin wants us to think they would have gone along with him and his friends if Malcolm hadn't frightened them.

Along with this indirect effect that Malcolm had on the civil rights organizations, he also had a direct effect—to push them to the left, to make them speak if not act more militantly, to make them demand more. Rustin knows about this. In fact, in 1961, when for a short while he favored collaboration between his wing of the movement and the black nationalists, he admitted about the latter: "And in crying out as they do and in swelling their ranks with the disenchanted and dispossessed, these groups are bringing increasing pressure to bear upon the integrationist organizations."[3] But Rustin has nothing to say about this effect after Malcolm's death—it doesn't really reflect credit on the civil rights organizations, or himself, to admit that Malcolm's pressure pushed them as much toward the left as they are.

If Malcolm's "help to the established civil rights organizations" earns the highest praise possible in Rustin's book, the smallness of Malcolm's organization is cited as one of his worst shortcomings. "But he never had many actual followers."(1) "But having blown the trumpet, he could summon, even at the very end, only a handful of followers." (2) Rustin likes this last sentence so much that he quotes it in the third article, and then adds: "Of course we cannot judge political effectiveness by numbers alone, but we cannot ignore his inability to build a movement."(3) But if effectiveness cannot be judged "by numbers alone," then why the constant harping on the smallness of Malcolm's organization? Is it only to reassure Rustin's white audience, or is it to reassure himself as well?

If Rustin cannot ignore Malcolm's alleged inability to build a movement (and no one has asked him to ignore it), then why doesn't he discuss it – who's stopping him? Let him reconcile this "inability" with his own remark earlier in the same article about the "qualities that made him a successful ghetto organizer" for Muhammad. Let him discuss, not ignore, the difficulties that faced Malcolm in building a new kind of movement. Let him explain why he thinks that Malcolm's 50 weeks of independence was a sufficient period for concluding that he suffered from an inability to build a movement. And let him, this time, try to explain what he has reported without apparently understanding: "One time at the Community Church in a debate I told him that his point of view led to jail, to exile or to assassination. He just laughed and called me Dr. Rustin."(1) A *revolutionary* movement, for which the price can indeed be jail, exile or assassination, is harder to build than Rustin's kind of movement.

"But having described the evil, he had no program for attacking it."(2) What Rustin means by this is that Malcolm did not have Rustin's program.* That, of course, is true –

---

* This is Rustin's standard criticism of anybody he disagrees with. He used to think CORE had a program, as long as it coincided with his own. But when CORE, after Malcolm's death, began to have new thoughts about black nationalism and to question some of the shibboleths about "integration," it was demoted by Rustin. At the June 1-2, 1966, White House conference on civil rights, when CORE director

Malcolm rejected the reformist strategy and politics of Rustin and the "Big Six." Rustin contends that the only alternative to his brand of gradualism is "passivity." It may be the only alternative that he can see, but it's not really the only one there is. Besides passivity, which Malcolm broke with Muhammad to get away from, Malcolm saw a revolutionary alternative to gradualism. That was what he was working on after the split. He was still assembling the component parts of such a program at the time of his death. It is true that Malcolm sometimes stated, with his customary modesty and honesty, that he did not have a program. What he meant was that he did not have a program yet, that his program was not yet completed. But an uncompleted program is not the same thing as "no program." Rustin admits as much, in another place, when he writes, "Till the end, his program was a maze of contradictions." (3)

Before examining the contradictions that Rustin sees in Malcolm's program, it is necessary to understand the general method that he uses in these three articles. Stated simply, it is to lump together the three different stages of Malcolm's life after he left prison – the Black Muslim, the transition and the final periods – as though they were a single period during which Malcolm's ideas remained constant or little changed. Literally 95 percent of the statements in these articles could have been written when Malcolm was a Black Muslim. Malcolm's evolution, as a process, is thus blurred or blotted out. The picture that comes through is that of Malcolm the Black Muslim, with a few features indistinct or unclear. No better method could be devised for making Malcolm's legacy "ambiguous."

Of course Rustin mentions the split and the fact that Malcolm's position changed on certain questions, but these are in the nature of unimportant asides, either vague or

Floyd McKissick argued that resolutions should be voted on as well as discussed, "Rustin scoffed at the spat over resolutions and called the CORE demand 'an indication of what an organization without a program will do to get on the front pages.'"4 When SNCC and CORE advanced the concept of "black power" in the summer of 1966, Rustin "passed off black power as 'just another slogan for those who don't have a program.'" 5

abstract; they cover Rustin technically, but they have no relation to his preceding and subsequent adverse judgments. For example: "There is evidence that toward the end Malcolm was seeking a new role for himself, that his theological (for lack of a better word) views were changing, that his hostility to whites was becoming less absolute, and that he was turning his attention to the possibilities of political action. What *kind* of political action is uncertain." (2) "Before his death he was working toward a more creative approach to the problems of the ghetto." (3)

The new role that Malcolm was seeking was that of a revolutionary – he had started "messing with the system," as David Llorens puts it [6]; why is Rustin afraid to say it? Malcolm was thinking about working with militant whites; why doesn't Rustin state it like that, clearly and simply, instead of saying grudgingly that "his hostility to whites was becoming less absolute"? There was nothing uncertain about the kind of political action Malcolm was becoming interested in – it was independent political action, it was political action against the two-party system; why does Rustin so sedulously avoid, in all three articles, quoting Malcolm's bitter condemnations of the Democratic Party and his call on the black people to break with that party? Why doesn't he find room to mention the fact that in September, 1964, Malcolm was tempted to leave what he considered vital business in Africa to return to the United States and run as the Michigan Freedom Now Party's candidate for the U. S. Senate? And why doesn't he have one concrete word about Malcolm's "more creative approach" to ghetto problems? Because to do these things would invalidate his three articles from beginning to end. He is silent about Malcolm's final positions, deliberately silent, because if he acknowledged them he would have little or nothing to write.

One of Rustin's strongest and apparently most telling criticisms of Malcolm – for his "economics" – is also one of the best examples of his general method. With the sophistication acquired by many years around the radical movement, Rustin sneers at Malcolm's naivete in "advocating that Negroes pool their resources into small business establishments at a time when small business enterprises are declining under the pressure of big business . . . It was as if Malcolm refused to understand the radical changes the current technological revolution is creating in the structure of the national economy."(2) "In short, Malcolm's economic program was not radical. It was, in fact, petty bourgeois."(3) The impression Rustin leaves is that this was Malcolm's position always, at the end as well as the beginning of his public life.

As a Black Muslim, Malcolm shared the resentment that most Negroes feel about white control of the shops and other businesses in black neighborhoods and supported the demand that black people should own and control the businesses in their community. When he left the Black Muslims he carried this position along with him, almost automatically, and raised the demand for black-owned businesses in the transition period. But it is important to recall here that Malcolm at first held a separatist perspective in the transition period, and to add that this separatist perspective was directly and closely connected with his ideas about black ownership of business. The connection can be seen clearly in the following passage from the phonograph record, "Malcolm X Speaks Again," which was prepared early in the transition period – in the last week of March or the first week of April, 1964 – although it was not released until after his death:

> The economic philosophy of black nationalism only means that our people need to be re-educated into the importance of controlling the economy of our community, controlling the economy of the community in which we live. And controlling the economy of the community in which we live means that we have to learn how to own and operate the businesses of our community and develop them into some type of industry that will enable us to create employment for the people of our community so that they won't have to constantly be involved in picketing and boycotting other people in other communities in order to get a job.
>
> Also, in line with this economic philosophy of black nationalism, in order for us to control the economy of our own community, we have to learn the importance of spending our money in the community where we live.

Anyone who knows the basic principles of economics must be aware of the fact that when you take the money out of the neighborhood in which you live and spend it in an integrated neighborhood – or rather, in your effort to integrate, you spend it in a neighborhood in which you don't live – the neighborhood in which you spend your money becomes wealthier and wealthier, and the neighborhood out of which you take your money becomes poorer and poorer. And this is one of the reasons why wherever you find Negroes, a slum condition usually develops, or we have to live in the ghetto – because all our wealth is spent elsewhere.

And even when we try to spend the money in the neighborhood where we live, usually, because we haven't learned the importance of owning and operating businesses, the businesses of our community are usually also controlled by outsiders, the stores are controlled by people who don't even live in our community. So even when we try and spend our money in the neighborhood where we live, we're spending it with someone who puts it in a basket and takes it out as soon as the sun goes down.

So the economic philosophy of black nationalism puts the burden upon the black man of learning how to control his own economy. . . .

Just as it took nationalism to bring about the independence of our brothers and sisters in Africa and Asia, the goal or the objective of the political, social and economic philosophy of black nationalism is designed to bring about the complete independence of the black people in this country by making us become consciously involved in controlling our own community. *Once we can control our own communities now, then perhaps we will later be able to control our own country, control our own nation, and govern ourselves and in some way have control over our own destiny.* . . . This philosophy in itself will bring about the independent thinking of the black people in this country, and eventually lead to the complete physical independence of the black people in this country.[7] (My emphasis – G. B.)

Did Malcolm continue to hold these ideas after the transition period (as one might think from reading Rustin)? The answer, very definitely, is no. As he gave up advocacy of a separate black nation, he also began to reconsider the question of black-owned business as a solution to the economic plight of the black people.

Thus, in the June 28, 1964 "Statement of Basic Aims and Objectives of the Organization of Afro-American Unity," the section on economics does *not* advocate Negro-owned businesses. It pledges that the OAAU will wage an unrelenting struggle against all forms of economic exploitation and discrimination, but nowhere does it advocate black businesses as the answer. The closest it comes to that is in two sentences about the rights of veterans, where it asserts that "The Afro-American veteran must be aware of all the [government] benefits due him and the procedure for obtaining them. These veterans must be encouraged to go into business together, using G. I. loans, etc." But advising veterans to go into business together is not the same thing that Rustin attributes to Malcolm.

Similarly, in the February 15, 1965 "Basic Unity Program of the Organization of Afro-American Unity" there is no mention whatever of Negro-owned businesses (not even by veterans). The closest thing to it, in the section on economic security, is the pledge that one of the OAAU's "measures to free our people from economic slavery . . . will be to maintain a Technician Pool: that is, a Bank of Technicians. In the same manner that blood banks have been established to furnish blood to those who need it at the time it is needed, we must establish a Technician Bank. We must do this so that the newly independent nations of Africa can turn to us who are their Afro-American brothers for the technicians they will need now and in the future. Thereby, we will be developing an open market for the many skills we possess and at the same time we will be supplying Africa with the skills she can best use. This project will therefore be one of mutual cooperation and mutual benefit." A pool of technicians will not free the black people from economic exploitation and dependence, but it is not at all the kind of program Rustin would have us believe Malcolm held from beginning to end.*

---

* The "Basic Unity Program" also does not contain anything like the project announced on June 15, 1966, by Ella Collins, Malcolm's sister and successor as chairman of the OAAU. According to the UPI, Mrs. Collins said that the OAAU planned to establish a black com-

In other words, Rustin is playing a trick on his readers. It is the same kind of trick that we could play on him if, in an article purporting to sum up his views, we discussed the pro-Marxist sympathies he had many years ago when he was a young man, and "forgot" to mention that he later rejected and repudiated those ideas most decisively. If Rustin told the whole story, he would have to add that in Malcolm's final period he began to advocate socialism and world revolution as the answer to the needs of American Negroes and their brothers abroad. Of course if he did that, it would be harder for him to liken Malcolm to the conservative Booker T. Washington. Why spoil a good polemic with facts?

The same defect can be seen in Rustin's statement that Malcolm "never clearly understood that as progress was made toward social integration, the problem for America's Negroes would become just as much one of class as of race."(3) If Malcolm "never" clearly understood the class aspects of the struggle, then how was he able to tell Pierre Berton on January 19, 1965, that he believed "there will be a clash between those who want freedom, justice and equality for everyone and those who want to continue the systems of exploitation . . . but I don't think that it will be based upon the color of the skin"? Or how could he tell an audience at Columbia University on February 18, 1965, "It is incorrect to classify the revolt of the Negro as simply a racial conflict of black against white, or as a purely American problem. Rather, we are today seeing a global rebellion of the oppressed against the oppressor, of the exploited against the exploiter"? No, the Malcolm of Rustin's articles is not the Malcolm who lived, learned and grew in real life, right down to his last hour.

A fair commentator not only has the obligation to show where, how and why Malcolm's ideas changed – he also has to take into account the fact that Malcolm did not always have the time or opportunity to state or restate his

munity, to be called "The Garden of Eden," on 1,000 acres of land near Albany. She said 250 black people would move into the community, which would include farms, schools and homes, and that this was the start of a ten-year program to establish such projects throughout the country.

ideas precisely; that is, he must not be content with this or that passing formulation but must seek to throw light on Malcolm's *intention*. This is the opposite of what Rustin does. His main concern is with striking at weak points in some of Malcolm's formulations. As an opponent of Malcolm he has the right to do this, of course; but the result is one-sided, only part of the truth and not the truth itself. Thus, for example, Rustin seizes on some unfortunate and overgenerous remarks Malcolm made about Prince Faisal, who had shown Malcolm extraordinary courtesies in an emotionally tense period during his trip to Mecca, and he writes: "Nor should it be surprising that the Negro masses did not support his proposed alliance of black Americans, Africans, and Arabs, including such leaders as Prince Faisal. For what did a Harlem Negro, let alone an Arab Bedouin, have in common with a feudal prince like Faisal?'[3] Malcolm did fail, on occasion, to differentiate sufficiently between revolutionary and nonrevolutionary African, Arab and Asian leaders, and for this he is certainly subject to criticism. But Rustin isn't satisfied to make that sort of criticism, however severely, and then relate it to the rest of Malcolm's thinking about alliances. He just stops there and says nothing whatever about the rest, including the relevant fact that the character of the international alliances Malcolm projected for Afro-Americans was revolutionary and anti-imperialist if it was anything.

"Malcolm," says Rustin, "strove to retrieve the Negro's shattered manhood from the wreckage of slavery, from the debris of matriarchy and family instability, from poverty and narcotics, from conditioned aimlessness, self-hatred and chaos. He could not succeed because these are not problems that can be exorcised by religious mysticism or denunciatory rhetoric. What is required is a strategy for social change, and Malcolm was not willing (except perhaps when it was too late) to abandon premises which had made him and his program a maze of contradictions."[2]

The parenthetical "except perhaps when it was too late" is typical Rustinese. He can "clear" himself by pointing to it, and that is its only purpose. What he implies and what he means is that Malcolm obstinately held on to premises that prevented him from developing a strategy for social change. Yet a little later in the same article Rustin admits that Malcolm did have such a strategy, although of course he distorts it almost beyond recognition: "Malcolm X was a child of the ghetto and he was dedicated to the preservation of the ghetto, which he thought could either be transformed from within or transplanted to a happier environment. That was his central error, and he cannot be easily forgiven for it . . . The movement we build, while deriving from the ghetto, must be dedicated to its destruction."(2)

Translated, what Rustin is talking about is this: Malcolm believed that the liberation of the Negro people is, first and foremost, the task of the Negro people themselves; that this task cannot be accomplished without the mobilization of the black masses, who are locked into the ghetto; and that the ghetto masses cannot be mobilized to transform the condition of their lives by any "compromising"* approach or by methods acceptable to middle-class Negroes. Malcolm understood that Afro-Americans need allies, and he expected that they would get allies, both at home and abroad. But he did not believe that they would get the right allies, or get allies on the right basis, until they were

---

* Rustin's comrade, Irving Howe, has no sympathy for Malcolm's attitude to "compromise": "Malcolm, intransigent in words and nihilistic in reality, never invoked the possibility or temptations of immediate struggle; he never posed the problems, confusions and risks of maneuver, compromise, retreat. Brilliantly Malcolm spoke for a rejection so complete it transformed him into an apolitical spectator, or in the language his admirers are more inclined to use than I am, a pure 'cop-out.'"8 Whatever kernels of truth may be lodged in these remarks apply exclusively to Malcolm the Black Muslim, not to the Malcolm who was trying to build a new movement that would engage in the immediate struggle. If Malcolm had lived, he would surely have faced "the problems, confusions and risks of maneuver, compromise and retreat" – although not, we can be certain, in the manner of the Howe-Rustin school, whose prime characteristic is compromise as principle, not compromise as tactic. "Uncompromising" was one of Malcolm's key words. Leon Trotsky recalled in his autobiography that "the words 'irreconcilable' and 'relentless' are among Lenin's favorites." Malcolm meant by "uncompromising" exactly what Lenin meant by "irreconcilable." The Russian Howes and Rustins of 1917 thought Lenin was a nihilistic cop-out because he would not go along with them in compromising with the liberal capitalists and supporting or joining their government.

strongly and solidly organized in a militant movement of their own. When they were organized in the right way, the right kinds of alliances would follow; and so would the right kind of social change. Hence Malcolm's "strategy for social change" was directed at the *first* link in this chain— the independent mobilization of the black people, which he hoped would include a section of the middle-class Negroes but which he believed would have to be based primarily on the black masses in the ghetto. Whatever facilitated this mobilization, including the language and methods that are called black nationalist, was good; whatever hampered it was bad; and whatever had no effect on it one way or another was, for the time being, irrelevant.

This strategy is radically different from Rustin's, Martin Luther King's and Roy Wilkins'. Theirs flows from the *dependence* of Negroes on liberal and moderate allies in the government, labor bureaucracy, churches, and so on. This dependence compels them to accept the role of adjunct and auxiliary, and to limit their demands to those sanctioned by their allies. As a result, not only their demands but all their actions, their very style, are and must be basically liberal and middle class. This is why they have been unable to get any kind of following in the ghetto, which is Malcolm territory.

Malcolm's strategy points in a revolutionary direction, Rustin's cannot go beyond gradualism and reform. The future of the United States will depend in great part on which one is ultimately chosen and acted on by the mass of the people in the black ghetto. The growth of mass sympathy and support exhibited in the summer of 1966 for the SNCC-CORE concept of "black power" indicates that the tide is turning away from Rustin's course and toward Malcolm's.

The difference is pointed up by one last statement from Rustin's polemics: "White America, not the Negro people, will determine Malcolm's role in history."(1) It is a revealing remark. Unconsciously almost, it expresses the deeply-rooted conviction of the Rustins that the black people are, and will remain, impotent and helpless—unable even to have heroes of their own without white permission. This conviction, which American capitalism seeks to reinforce in every possible way, is the root of the Rustin-King-Wilkins strategy too. If the black masses accept Rustin's strategy, then white America will indeed determine Malcolm's place in history, and it won't be a favorable one—because white America will not be fundamentally changed that way. But if they adopt Malcolm's strategy, accept his legacy and develop it in accord with the logic of the direction in which he was moving during his last year, then all of America will be transformed through the struggles that will be initiated by black radicals, and the day will come when all decent Americans will look back on Malcolm with gratitude and love.

Malcolm X

Photo by Laurence Henry

"Take my picture by this sign," Malcolm told Laurence Henry. "I like it."

Photo by Laurence Henry

Clifton DeBerry and Malcolm X at Militant Labor Forum in New York. DeBerry, chairman of the meeting, was the Socialist Workers Party's Presidential candidate in 1964.

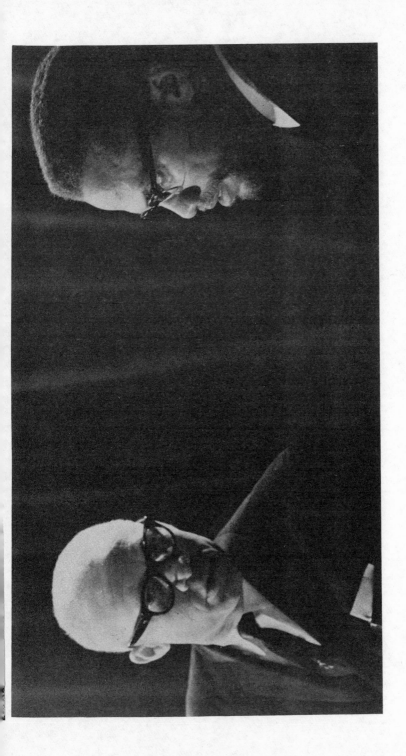

Discussion with members of audience after meeting's adjournment.

Appendix A

Statement of Basic Aims and Objectives
Of the Organization of Afro-American Unity*

The Organization of Afro-American Unity, organized and structured by a cross-section of the Afro-American people living in the U.S.A., has been patterned after the letter and spirit of the Organization of African Unity established at Addis Ababa, Ethiopia, May, 1963.

We, the members of the Organization of Afro-American Unity gathered together in Harlem, New York:

Convinced that it is the inalienable right of all people to control their own destiny;

Conscious of the fact that freedom, equality, justice and dignity are essential objectives for the achievement of the legitimate aspirations of the people of African descent here in the Western Hemisphere, we will endeavor to build a bridge of understanding and create the basis for Afro-American unity;

Conscious of our responsibility to harness the natural and human resources of our people for their total advancement in all spheres of human endeavor;

Inspired by a common determination to promote understanding among our people and co-operation in all matters pertaining to their survival and advancement, we will support the aspirations of our people for brotherhood and solidarity in a larger unity transcending all organizational differences;

Convinced that, in order to translate this determination into a dynamic force in the cause of human progress, conditions of peace and security must be established and maintained;

Determined to unify the Americans of African descent in their fight for human rights and dignity, and being fully aware that this is not possible in the present atmosphere

---

* Dated June 28, 1964.

and condition of oppression, we dedicate ourselves to the building of a political, economic, and social system of justice and peace;

Dedicated to the unification of all people of African descent in this hemisphere and to the utilization of that unity to bring into being the organizational structure that will project the black people's contributions to the world;

Persuaded that the Charter of the United Nations, the Universal Declaration of Human Rights, the Constitution of the U.S.A. and the Bill of Rights are the principles in which we believe and these documents if put into practice represent the essence of mankind's hopes and good intentions;

Desirous that all Afro-American people and organizations should henceforth unite so that the welfare and well-being of our people will be assured;

Resolved to reinforce the common bond of purpose between our people by submerging all of our differences and establishing a non-religious and non-sectarian constructive program for human rights;

Do hereby present this charter.

I – Establishment

The Organization of Afro-American Unity shall include all people of African descent in the Western Hemisphere, as well as our brothers and sisters on the African Continent.

II – Self-Defense

Since self-preservation is the first law of nature, we assert the Afro-American's right of self-defense.

The Constitution of the U.S.A. clearly affirms the right of every American citizen to bear arms. And as Americans, we will not give up a single right guaranteed under the Constitution. The history of the unpunished violence against our people clearly indicates that we must be prepared to defend ourselves or we will continue to be a defenseless people at the mercy of a ruthless and violent racist mob.

We assert that in those areas where the government is

either unable or unwilling to protect the lives and property of our people, that our people are within their rights to protect themselves by whatever means necessary. A man with a rifle or club can only be stopped by a person who defends himself with a rifle or club.

Tactics based solely on morality can only succeed when you are dealing with basically moral people or a moral system. A man or system which oppresses a man because of his color is not moral. It is the duty of every Afro-American and every Afro-American community throughout this country to protect its people against mass murderers, bombers, lynchers, floggers, brutalizers and exploiters.

III – Education

Education is an important element in the struggle for human rights. It is the means to help our children and people rediscover their identity and thereby increase self-respect. Education is our passport to the future, for tomorrow belongs to the people who prepare for it today.

Our children are being criminally shortchanged in the public school system of America. The Afro-American schools are the poorest run schools in New York City. Principals and teachers fail to understand the nature of the problems with which they work and as a result they cannot do the job of teaching our children. The textbooks tell our children nothing about the great contributions of Afro-Americans to the growth and development of this country. The Board of Education's integration program is expensive and unworkable; and the organization of principals and supervisors in the New York City school system has refused to support the Board's plan to integrate the schools, thus dooming it to failure.

The Board of Education has said that even with its plan there are ten per cent of the schools in the Harlem-Bedford-Stuyvesant community they cannot improve. This means that the Organization of Afro-American Unity must make the Afro-American community a more potent force for educational self-improvement.

A first step in the program to end the existing system of

racist education is to demand that the ten per cent of the schools the Board of Education will not include in its plan be turned over to and run by the Afro-American community. We want Afro-American principals to head these schools. We want Afro-American teachers in these schools. We want textbooks written by Afro-Americans that are acceptable to us to be used in these schools.

The Organization of Afro-American Unity will select and recommend people to serve on local school boards where school policy is made and passed on to the Board of Education.

Through these steps we will make the ten per cent of schools we take over educational showplaces that will attract the attention of people all over the nation.

If these proposals are not met, we will ask Afro-American parents to keep their children out of the present inferior schools they attend. When these schools in our neighborhood are controlled by Afro-Americans, we will return to them.

The Organization of Afro-American Unity recognizes the tremendous importance of the complete involvement of Afro-American parents in every phase of school life. Afro-American parents must be willing and able to go into the schools and see that the job of educating our children is done properly.

We call on all Afro-Americans around the nation to be aware that the conditions that exist in the New York City public school system are as deplorable in their cities as they are here. We must unite our effort and spread our program of self-improvement through education to every Afro-American community in America.

We must establish all over the country schools of our own to train our children to become scientists and mathematicians. We must realize the need for adult education and for job retraining programs that will emphasize a changing society in which automation plays the key role. We intend to use the tools of education to help raise our people to an unprecedented level of excellence and self-respect through their own efforts.

IV – Politics – Economics

Basically, there are two kinds of power that count in America: economic and political, with social power deriving from the two. In order for the Afro-Americans to control their destiny, they must be able to control and affect the decisions which control their destiny: economic, political and social. This can only be done through organization.

The Organization of Afro-American Unity will organize the Afro-American community block by block to make the community aware of its power and potential; we will start immediately a voter-registration drive to make every unregistered voter in the Afro-American community an independent voter; we propose to support and/or organize political clubs, to run independent candidates for office, and to support any Afro-American already in office who answers to and is responsible to the Afro-American community.

Economic exploitation in the Afro-American community is the most vicious form practiced on any people in America; twice as much rent for rat-infested, roach-crawling, rotting tenements; the Afro-American pays more for foods, clothing, insurance rates and so forth. The Organization of Afro-American Unity will wage an unrelenting struggle against these evils in our community. There shall be organizers to work with the people to solve these problems, and start a housing self-improvement program. We propose to support rent strikes and other activities designed to better the community.

V – Social

This organization is responsible only to the Afro-American people and community and will function only with their support, both financially and numerically. We believe that our communities must be the sources of their own strength politically, economically, intellectually and culturally in the struggle for human rights and dignity.

The community must reinforce its moral responsibility to rid itself of the effects of years of exploitation, neglect and apathy, and wage an unrelenting struggle against police brutality.

The Afro-American community must accept the responsibility for regaining our people who have lost their place in society. We must declare an all-out war on organized crime in our community; a vice that is controlled by policemen who accept bribes and graft, and who must be exposed. We must establish a clinic, whereby one can get aid and cure for drug addiction; and create meaningful, creative, useful activities for those who were led astray down the avenues of vice.

The people of the Afro-American community must be prepared to help each other in all ways possible; we must establish a place where unwed mothers can get help and advice; a home for the aged in Harlem and an orphanage in Harlem.

We must set up a guardian system that will help our youth who get into trouble and also provide constructive activities for our children. We must set a good example for our children and must teach them to always be ready to accept the responsibilities that are necessary for building good communities and nations. We must teach them that their greatest responsibilities are to themselves, to their families and to their communities.

The Organization of Afro-American Unity believes that the Afro-American community must endeavor to do the major part of all charity work from within the community. Charity, however, does not mean that to which we are legally entitled in the form of government benefits. The Afro-American veteran must be made aware of all the benefits due him and the procedure for obtaining them. These veterans must be encouraged to go into business together, using G. I. loans, etc.

Afro-Americans must unite and work together. We must take pride in the Afro-American community, for it is home and it is power.

What we do here in regaining our self-respect, manhood, dignity and freedom helps all people everywhere who are fighting against oppression.

VI – Culture

"A race of people is like an individual man; until it uses its own talent, takes pride in its own history, expresses its own culture, affirms its own selfhood, it can never fulfill itself."

Our history and our culture were completely destroyed when we were forcibly brought to America in chains. And now it is important for us to know that our history did not begin with slavery's scars. We come from Africa, a great continent and a proud and varied people, a land which is the new world and was the cradle of civilization. Our culture and our history are as old as man himself and yet we know almost nothing of it. We must recapture our heritage and our identity if we are ever to liberate ourselves from the bonds of white supremacy. We must launch a cultural revolution to unbrainwash an entire people.

Our cultural revolution must be the means of bringing us closer to our African brothers and sisters. It must begin in the community and be based on community participation. Afro-Americans will be free to create only when they can depend on the Afro-American community for support and Afro-American artists must realize that they depend on the Afro-American for inspiration. We must work toward the establishment of a cultural center in Harlem, which will include people of all ages, and will conduct workshops in all the arts, such as film, creative writing, painting, theater, music, Afro-American history, etc.

This cultural revolution will be the journey to our rediscovery of ourselves. History is a people's memory, and without a memory man is demoted to the lower animals.

Armed with the knowledge of the past, we can with confidence charter a course for our future. Culture is an indispensable weapon in the freedom struggle. We must take hold of it and forge the future with the past.

* * *

When the battle is won, let history be able to say to each one of us: "He was a dedicated patriot: *Dignity* was his country, *Manhood* was his government, and *Freedom* was his land." (from *And Then We Heard the Thunder,* by John Oliver Killens)

Appendix B

Basic Unity Program
Organization of Afro-American Unity

Pledging unity . . .
Promoting justice . . .
Transcending compromise . . .
We, Afro-Americans, people who originated in Africa and
now reside in America, speak out against the slavery and
oppression inflicted upon us by this racist power structure.
We offer to downtrodden Afro-American people courses of
action that will conquer oppression, relieve suffering and
convert meaningless struggle into meaningful action.

Confident that our purpose will be achieved, we Afro-
Americans from all walks of life make the following known:

Establishment

Having stated our determination, confidence and resolve,
the Organization of Afro-American Unity is hereby established on the 15th day of February, 1965, in the city of
New York.

Upon this establishment, we Afro-American people will
launch a cultural revolution which will provide the means
for restoring our identity that we might rejoin our brothers
and sisters on the African continent, culturally, psychologically, economically and share with them the sweet fruits of
freedom from oppression and independence of racist gov-
ernments.

1. The Organization of Afro-American Unity welcomes
all persons of African origin to come together and dedicate
their ideas, skills and lives to free our people from oppression.

2. Branches of the Organization of Afro-American Unity
may be established by people of African descent wherever
they may be and whatever their ideology – as long as they
be descendants of Africa and dedicated to our one goal:

Freedom from oppression.

3. The basic program of the Organization of Afro-American Unity which is now being presented can and will be modified by the membership, taking into consideration national, regional and local conditions that require flexible treatment.

4. The Organization of Afro-American Unity encourages active participation of each member since we feel that each and every Afro-American has something to contribute to our freedom. Thus each member will be encouraged to participate in the committee of his or her choice.

5. Understanding the differences that have been created amongst us by our oppressors in order to keep us divided, the Organization of Afro-American Unity strives to ignore or submerge these artificial divisions by focusing our activities and our loyalties upon our one goal: Freedom from oppression.

Basic Aims and Objectives

Self-determination

We assert that we Afro-Americans have the right to direct and control our lives, our history and our future rather than to have our destinies determined by American racists . . .

We are determined to rediscover our true African culture which was crushed and hidden for over four hundred years in order to enslave us and keep us enslaved up to today . . .

We, Afro-Americans – enslaved, oppressed and denied by a society that proclaims itself the citadel of democracy, are determined to rediscover our history, promote the talents that are suppressed by our racist enslavers, renew the culture that was crushed by a slave government and thereby – to again become a free people.

National Unity

Sincerely believing that the future of Afro-Americans is dependent upon our ability to unite our ideas, skills, organizations and institutions . . .

We, the Organization of Afro-American Unity pledge to join hands and hearts with all people of African origin in a grand alliance by forgetting all the differences that the power structure has created to keep us divided and enslaved. We further pledge to strengthen our common bond and strive toward one goal: Freedom from oppression.

The Basic Unity Program

The program of the Organization of Afro-American Unity shall evolve from five strategic points which are deemed basic and fundamental to our grand alliance. Through our committees we shall proceed in the following general areas:

I. Restoration

In order to enslave the African it was necessary for our enslavers to completely sever our communications with the African continent and the Africans that remained there. In order to free ourselves from the oppression of our enslavers then, it is absolutely necessary for the Afro-American to restore communications with Africa.

The Organization of Afro-American Unity will accomplish this goal by means of independent national and international newspapers, publishing ventures, personal contacts and other available communications media.

We, Afro-Americans, must also communicate to one another the truths about American slavery and the terrible effects it has upon our people. We must study the modern system of slavery in order to free ourselves from it. We must search out all the bare and ugly facts without shame for we are still victims, still slaves – still oppressed. Our only shame is believing falsehood and not seeking the truth.

We must learn all that we can about ourselves. We will have to know the whole story of how we were kidnapped from Africa, how our ancestors were brutalized, dehumanized and murdered and how we are continually kept in a state of slavery for the profit of a system conceived in slavery, built by slaves and dedicated to keeping us enslaved in order to maintain itself.

We must begin to reeducate ourselves and become alert listeners in order to learn as much as we can about the

progress of our Motherland–Africa. We must correct in
our minds the distorted image that our enslaver has por-
trayed to us of Africa that he might discourage us from
reestablishing communications with her and thus obtain
freedom from oppression.

II. Reorientation

In order to *keep* the Afro-American enslaved, it was
necessary to limit our thinking to the shores of America–
to prevent us from identifying our problems with the problems of other peoples of African origin. This made us consider ourselves an isolated minority without allies anywhere.

The Organization of Afro-American Unity will develop
in the Afro-American people a keen awareness of our relationship with the world at large and clarify our roles,
rights and responsibilities as human beings. We can accomplish this goal by becoming well informed concerning
world affairs and understanding that our struggle is part
of a larger world struggle of oppressed peoples against
all forms of oppression. We must change the thinking of
the Afro-American by liberating our minds through the
study of philosophies and psychologies, cultures and languages that did not come from our racist oppressors. Pro-
visions are being made for the study of languages such as
Swahili, Hausa and Arabic. These studies will give our
people access to ideas and history of mankind at large and
thus increase our mental scope.

We can learn much about Africa by reading informative
books and by listening to the experiences of those who
have traveled there, but many of us can travel to the land
of our choice and experience for ourselves. The Organization of Afro-American Unity will encourage the Afro-American to travel to Africa, the Caribbean and to other places
where our culture has not been completely crushed by brutality and ruthlessness.

III. Education

After enslaving us, the slavemasters developed a racist
educational system which justified to its posterity the evil
deeds that had been committed against the African people

and their descendants. Too often the slave himself partici-
pates so completely in this system that he justifies having
been enslaved and oppressed.

The Organization of Afro-American Unity will devise
original educational methods and procedures which will
liberate the minds of our children from the vicious lies
and distortions that are fed to us from the cradle to keep
us mentally enslaved. We encourage Afro-Americans themselves to establish experimental institutes and educational
workshops, liberation schools and child-care centers in
the Afro-American communities.

We will influence the choice of textbooks and equipment
used by our children in the public schools while at the same
time encouraging qualified Afro-Americans to write and
publish the textbooks needed to liberate our minds. Until
we completely control our own educational institutions, we
must supplement the formal training of our children by
educating them at home.

IV. Economic Security

After the Emancipation Proclamation, when the system of
slavery changed from chattel slavery to wage slavery, it
was realized that the Afro-American constituted the largest
homogeneous ethnic group with a common origin and
common group experience in the United States and, if
allowed to exercise economic or political freedom, would
in a short period of time own this country. Therefore racists in this government developed techniques that would
keep the Afro-American people economically dependent
upon the slavemasters – economically slaves – twentieth century slaves.

The Organization of Afro-American Unity will take measures to free our people from economic slavery. One way
of accomplishing this will be to maintain a Technician
Pool: that is, a Bank of Technicians. In the same manner
that blood banks have been established to furnish blood
to those who need it at the time it is needed, we must establish a Technician Bank. We must do this so that the
newly independent nations of Africa can turn to us who are
their Afro-American brothers for the technicians they will
need now and in the future. Thereby, we will be developing

an open market for the many skills we possess and at the same time we will be supplying Africa with the skills she can best use. This project will therefore be one of mutual cooperation and mutual benefit.

V. Self-Defense

In order to enslave a people and keep them subjugated, their right to self-defense must be denied. They must be constantly terrorized, brutalized and murdered. These tactics of suppression have been developed to a new high by vicious racists whom the United States government seems unwilling or incapable of dealing with in terms of the law of this land. Before the Emancipation it was the black man who suffered humiliation, torture, castration, and murder. Recently our women and children, more and more, are becoming the victims of savage racists whose appetite for blood increases daily and whose deeds of depravity seem to be openly encouraged by all law enforcement agencies. Over 5,000 Afro-Americans have been lynched since the Emancipation Proclamation and not one murderer has been brought to justice!

The Organization of Afro-American Unity, being aware of the increased violence being visited upon the Afro-American and of the open sanction of this violence and murder by the police departments throughout this country and the federal agencies – do affirm our right and obligation to defend ourselves in order to survive as a people.

We encourage all Afro-Americans to defend themselves against the wanton attacks of racist aggressors whose sole aim is to deny us the guarantees of the United Nations Charter of Human Rights and of the Constitution of the United States.

The Organization of Afro-American Unity will take those private steps that are necessary to insure the survival of the Afro-American people in the face of racist aggression and the defense of our women and children. We are within our rights to see to it that the Afro-American people who fulfill their obligations to the United States government (we pay taxes and serve in the armed forces of this country like American citizens do) also exact from this government the obligations that it owes us as a people, or exact these obligations ourselves. Needless to say, among this number we include protection of certain inalienable rights such as life, liberty and the pursuit of happiness.

In areas where the United States government has shown itself unable and/or unwilling to bring to justice the racist oppressors, murderers, who kill innocent children and adults, the Organization of Afro-American Unity advocates that the Afro-American people insure ourselves that justice is done—whatever the price and *by any means necessary*.

National Concerns

General Terminologies:

We Afro-Americans feel receptive toward all peoples of goodwill. We are not opposed to multi-ethnic associations in any walk of life. In fact, we have had experiences which enable us to understand how unfortunate it is that human beings have been set apart or aside from each other because of characteristics known as "racial" characteristics.

However, Afro-Americans did not create the prejudiced background and atmosphere in which we live. And we must face the facts. A "racial" society does exist in stark reality, and not with equality for black people; so we who are non-white must meet the problems inherited from centuries of inequalities and deal with the present situations as rationally as we are able.

The exclusive ethnic quality of our unity is necessary for self-preservation. We say this because: Our experiences backed up by history show that African culture and Afro-American culture will not be accurately recognized and reported and cannot be respectably expressed nor be secure in its survival if we remain the divided, and therefore the helpless, victims of an oppressive society.

We appreciate the fact that when the people involved have real equality and justice, ethnic intermingling can be beneficial to all. We must denounce, however, all people who are oppressive through their policies or actions and who are lacking in justice in their dealings with other people, whether the injustices proceed from power, class, or "race." We must be unified in order to be protected from abuse or misuse.

We consider the word "integration" a misleading, false term. It carries with it certain implications to which Afro-Americans cannot subscribe. This terminology has been applied to the current regulation projects which are supposedly "acceptable" to some classes of society. This very "acceptable" implies some inherent superiority or inferiority instead of acknowledging the true source of the inequalities involved.

We have observed that the usage of the term "integration" was designated and promoted by those persons who expect to continue a (nicer) type of ethnic discrimination and who intend to maintain social and economic control of all human contacts by means of imagery, classifications, quotas, and manipulations based on color, national origin, or "racial" background and characteristics.

Careful evaluation of recent experiences shows that "integration" actually describes the process by which a white society is (remains) set in a position to use, whenever it chooses to use and however it chooses to use, the best talents of non-white people. This power-web continues to build a society wherein the best contributions of Afro-Americans, in fact of all non-white people, would continue to be absorbed without note or exploited to benefit a fortunate few while the masses of both white and non-white people would remain unequal and unbenefited.

We are aware that many of us lack sufficient training and are deprived and unprepared as a result of oppression, discrimination, and the resulting discouragement, despair, and resignation. But when we are not qualified, and where we are unprepared, we must help each other and work out plans for bettering our own conditions as Afro-Americans. Then our assertions toward full opportunity can be made on the basis of equality as opposed to the calculated tokens of "integration." Therefore, we must reject this term as one used by all persons who intend to mislead Afro-Americans.

Another term, "negro," is erroneously used and is degrading in the eyes of informed and self-respecting persons of African heritage. It denotes stereotyped and debased traits of character and classifies a whole segment of humanity on the basis of false information. From all intelligent viewpoints, it is a badge of slavery and helps to prolong and perpetuate oppression and discrimination.

Persons who recognize the emotional thrust and plain show of disrespect in the southerner's use of "nigra" and the general use of "nigger" must also realize that all three words are essentially the same. The other two: "nigra" and "nigger" are blunt and undeceptive. The one representing respectability, "negro," is merely the same substance in a polished package and spelled with a capital letter. This refinement is added so that a degrading terminology can be legitimately used in general literature and "polite" conversation without embarrassment.

The term "negro" developed from a word in the Spanish language which is actually an adjective (describing word) meaning "black," that is, the *color* black. In plain English, if someone said or was called *A* "black" or *A* "dark," even a young child would very naturally question: "*A* black what?" or "*A* dark what?" because adjectives do not name, they describe. Please take note that in order to make use of this mechanism, a word was transferred from another language and deceptively changed in function from an adjective to a noun, which is a naming word. Its application in the nominative (naming) sense was intentionally used to portray persons in a position of objects or "things." It stamps the article as being "all alike and all the same." It denotes: a "darkie," a slave, a sub-human, an ex-slave, a "*negro*."

Afro-Americans must re-analyze and particularly question our own use of this term, keeping in mind all the facts. In light of the historical meanings and current implications, all intelligent and informed Afro-Americans and Africans continue to reject its use in the noun form as well as a proper adjective. Its usage shall continue to be considered as unenlightened and objectionable or deliberately offensive whether in speech or writing.

We accept the use of Afro-American, African, and Black Man in reference to persons of African heritage. To every other part of mankind goes this measure of just respect. We do not desire more nor shall we accept less.

General Considerations:

Afro-Americans, like all other people, have human rights which are inalienable. This is, these human rights cannot be legally or justly transferred *to* another. Our human rights belong to us, as to all people, through God, not through the wishes nor according to the whims of other men.

We must consider that fact and other reasons why a Proclamation of "Emancipation" should not be revered as a document of liberation. Any previous acceptance of and faith in such a document was based on sentiment, not on reality. This is a serious matter which we Afro-Americans must continue to re-evaluate.

The original root-meaning of the word *emancipation* is: "To deliver up or make over as property by means of a formal act from a purchaser." We must take note and remember that human beings cannot be *justly* bought or sold nor can their human rights be *legally* or justly taken away.

Slavery was, and still is, a criminal institution, that is: crime en masse. No matter what form it takes: subtle rules and policies, apartheid, etc., slavery and oppression of human rights stand as major crimes against God and humanity. Therefore, to relegate or change the state of such criminal deeds by means of vague legislation and noble euphemisms gives an honor to horrible commitments that is totally inappropriate.

Full implications and concomitant harvests were generally misunderstood by our foreparents and are still misunderstood or avoided by some Afro-Americans today. However, the facts remain; and we, as enlightened Afro-Americans, will not praise and encourage any belief in "emancipation." Afro-Americans everywhere must realize that to retain faith in such an idea means acceptance of being property and, therefore, less than a human being. This matter is a crucial one that Afro-Americans must continue to re-examine.

World-Wide Concerns

The time is past due for us to internationalize the problems of Afro-Americans. We have been too slow in recognizing the link in the fate of Africans with the fate of Afro-Americans. We have been too unknowing to understand and too misdirected to ask our African brothers and sisters to help us mend the chain of our heritage.

Our African relatives who are in a majority in their own country have found it very difficult to gain independence from a minority: It is that much more difficult for Afro-Americans who are a minority away from the motherland and still oppressed by those who encourage the crushing of our African identity.

We can appreciate the material progress and recognize the opportunities available in the highly industrialized and affluent American society. Yet, we who are non-white face daily miseries resulting directly or indirectly from a systematic discrimination against us because of our God-given colors. These factors cause us to remember that our being born in America was an act of fate stemming from the separation of our foreparents from Africa; not by choice, but by force.

We have for many years been divided among ourselves through deceptions and misunderstandings created by our enslavers, but we do here and now express our desires and intent to draw closer and be restored in knowledge and spirit through renewed relations and kinships with the African peoples. We further realize that our human rights, so long suppressed, are the rights of all mankind everywhere.

In light of all of our experiences and knowledge of the past, we, as Afro-Americans, declare recognition, sympathy, and admiration for all peoples and nations who are striving, as we are, toward self-realization and complete freedom from oppression!

The Civil Rights Bill is a similarly misleading, misinterpreted document of legislation. The premise of its design and application is not respectable in the eyes of men who recognize what personal freedom involves and entails. Afro-Americans must answer this question for themselves: What makes this special bill necessary?

The only document that is in order and deserved with regard to the acts perpetuated through slavery and oppression prolonged to this day is a *Declaration of Condemnation*. And the only legislation worthy of consideration or endorsement by Afro-Americans, the victims of these tragic institutions, is a *Proclamation of Restitution*. We Afro-Americans must keep these facts ever in mind.

We must continue to internationalize our philosophies and contacts toward assuming full human rights which include all the civil rights appertaining thereto. With complete understanding of our heritage as Afro-Americans, we must not do less.

———

Committees of the Organization of Afro-American Unity

The Cultural Committee
The Economic Committee
The Educational Committee
The Political Committee
The Publications Committee
The Social Committee
The Self-Defense Committee
The Youth Committee

Staff Committees

Finance   Fund-raising   Legal   Membership

For further information on the Organization of Afro-American Unity write:

Organization of Afro-American Unity
2090 Seventh Ave., Suite 128
New York 27, N.Y.

For speedier responses, address correspondence to a particular committee. For example, if you are interested in joining or establishing a chapter: Membership Committee, Organization of Afro-American Unity, 2090 Seventh Ave., Suite 128, New York 27, N.Y. We welcome your contributions in the form of checks or money orders.

Appendix C

The Rustin-Kahn Attack*
By Robert Vernon

There is always a reason why people attacked Malcolm X in life or in death. When civil rights liberals do this, they are expressing hostility to all black people who are not satisfied with and do not submit to "leadership" by white liberals or by Negroes fronting for white liberals. These adversaries of Malcolm X, and of all independent efforts by black people toward emancipation, are friends of the Negro, but enemies of black people.

The most sophisticated attack launched since the physical assassination of Malcolm X is an article by Bayard Rustin and Tom Kahn, two prominent "white liberals" (Rustin is Negro, but is difficult to distinguish from a white liberal in his politics, mentality, social outlook; in fact, he is in some respects more backward than the average white liberal), in the March 24 *New America,* the liberal periodical published by the Socialist Party. The importance attached to the attack is reflected in the fact that the article is reprinted under a different title in the Spring issue of *Dissent,* a liberal intellectual magazine for tired old radicals and tired young radicals.

If the liberals think this new attack is such great stuff, perhaps we might take a look at it, to see what their line of argument is, what good points they make, if any, and what cute tricks they employ to make their points.

Rustin and Kahn take as their main point: "Malcolm X was a child of the ghetto and he was dedicated to the preservation of the ghetto, which he thought could be either transformed from within or transplanted to a happier environment. That was his central error, and he cannot be easily forgiven it."

That isn't really the "central error," but they're getting

---

* Reprinted from *The Militant.* May 24 and May 31, 1965.

warm. Here we see a cute trick, that of presenting Malcolm X's views as identical with those of Elijah Muhammad, as if Malcolm X had done no thinking on his own, before or after the split with the Nation of Islam. Some liberals talk that way out of ignorance, but Rustin and Kahn know better.

The argument is asinine on the face of it. Malcolm X looked upon the black ghetto as a potential power base to be organized, with special problems which were not and are not being tackled by the liberal civil rights organizations. Now, big cities with their ghettos are where most of *us* live, so this is no minor point.

The vast majority of black people, North and South, are becoming concentrated in big city ghettos, not in isolated farm communities in the deep South, and the problems we face cannot be solved or even effectively tackled by the liberal civil rights approach developed for Southern rural life and for the Negro middle class. But to interpret the focusing of Malcolm X and other black rebels on the ghettos as an attempt to preserve the ghetto status quo is as ridiculous as criticizing a union organizer for trying to organize workers into a union instead of trying to *integrate* the production workers into the management front office.

The real "central error" committed by Malcolm X and other black militants, for which they "cannot be easily forgiven," is their refusal to submit to liberal "leadership" and to the Negro "leaders" propped up by the mass media, liberal money, and the friendly, smiling, non-racist part of the white power structure.

Let's get this much straight. There is nothing wrong with the Negro middle class having *its* organizations to fight for *its* immediate needs, to solve *its* problems by *its* methods and philosophy (including non-violent love, turn-the-other-cheek-ism, assimilation into the American Way of Life, the whole bit).

If the Negro middle class is quite satisfied with organizations financed by white liberal money, with many a white liberal gracing their boards of directors, and with policies designed not to offend liberals, that is *their* decision. They have a right to such organizations, allies, and

methods and goals of struggle. (Considering the millions
of dollars pumped annually into such organizations, the
support and guidance they get from the liberal power structure, the good press relations, the welcome mat at the
White House, etc., it is astounding *how little* these liberal
organizations achieve even for the Negro middle class!)

It would be nice, and would clear the air immensely, if
liberals and middle-class Negroes would then say: "We
are only interested in the problems of Negroes who seek
integration into this wonderful American Way of Life as it
is. If any Negroes have problems that cannot be solved
within the existing framework of American society, or that
cannot be solved by methods approved by us, by our white
liberal friends, and by our Great White Father in the White
House, then that is *their* problem!"

But life is not that simple. Liberals seek to control the
entire range of the Negro freedom struggle, to keep it
from getting out of hand, to moderate it, modulate it, straitjacket it in their own narrow, limited interests, keep it from
getting at the real problems. The preservation of the American Way of Life dictates that black people be kept safely
in restraint by liberal and middle-class "leadership."

It requires that liberal and middle-class "leadership" be
the only voice and representation not only of middle-class
Negroes, but of "the Negro," and this position must be for-
tified by generous funds, carefully-engineered opinion polls
asking the right questions, an occasional pat on the head
by Big Daddy in the White House, and even a Nobel Peace
Prize to a pacifist who fails to oppose the wars which his
own imperialist government is conducting.* It also requires
that independent black movements, organizations, and
leaders addressing themselves to the problems of black
people and seeking to build a power base independent of
the Negro middle class, independent of the liberal power
structure, be attacked, ridiculed, isolated if possible, even
persecuted, exiled, or assassinated.

An important part of the liberal attack developed by
Rustin and Kahn is that Malcolm X and, therefore, all
other black ghetto militants, offer nothing more than mere

---

*After this article, Rev. King began to make stronger statements
against the war in Vietnam. – G. B.

rhetoric, verbiage, a militant style or posture. "For all of his militancy, Malcolm was in many respects a conservative force in the Negro community. His violent rhetoric was a 'cop-out.'"

This line of attack is not demagogic, but meant sincerely. It goes over big with civil rights liberals. It rests on the assumption that the only "real" struggle is the civil rights integration struggle as defined by liberals, a narrow-minded assumption saturated with middle-class contempt and indifference toward the working-class black people in the urban ghettos (and, remember, that's most of *us!*).

Some ghetto rebels, equally narrow-minded, respond to this attitude with the absurd view that the struggle for civil rights and integration is phony and just a diversion from the "real" struggle. Neither one-sided view helps much. Both the civil rights - integration struggle and the black ghetto struggle are real, meaningful, and fruitful – and must be made more so.

They are not opposites, but interrelated, reflecting local differences and class differences. Any success achieved in one aspect of the struggle will aid the other; any defeat suffered in one is a defeat for the other. Malcolm X stressed this point, in fact; but you would never know about that from this article by Bayard Rustin and Tom Kahn.

More liberal narrow-mindedness shows up in the next barrage from Rustin and Kahn: "But whom did Malcolm really frighten? Surely not Goldwater, or Eastland or the racist power structure. Malcolm frightened and worried white liberals, those most in sympathy with the movement, and those with guilt-feelings."

Note carefully whom Rustin and Kahn single out as enemies. Not the power structure, but the *racist* power structure, i.e. Dixiecrats and others who oppose *civil rights* overtly. These certainly are enemies of black people, but they are not the *only* enemies we have in this God's country.

One conspicuous enemy of black people not listed here is His Imperial Highness, Architect of the Great Society Lyndon B. Johnson, Emperor of the Congo, South Vietnam, and the Dominican Republic, and Lord and Master of the Seven Seas and All Shores Adjacent Thereto. Eastland and Goldwater are not the ones who run this racist country, although they do have much to say. They could be considered *the* enemy only by liberals who are concerned exclusively with integration, civil rights, and assimilation of middle-class Negroes into this best of all possible societies.

But to put some substance into the freedom-now "revolution," some changes, deep-going changes, *revolutionary* changes will have to be brought about in the social, economic and political structure, and the movement to bring them about will have to be built. Liberal capitalist America is willing to throw out a few crumbs of integration and civil rights if enough noise and pressure are made, and if that will help keep things under control. There can even be a Great Society crumb or two to con the ghetto masses (but not much more—there isn't enough to go around even for poor whites).

But the "revolution" must not be allowed to fall into the wrong hands—into the hands of black people—any more than the revolution in Santo Domingo could be safely entrusted to the Dominican people.

How liberal capitalist America would respond to such a catastrophe is eloquently demonstrated by the artillery dug in around Santo Domingo, zeroed-in on the sections of the city freed by our Dominican black brothers. The napalm bombs dangling from the bays of U. S. jet bombers carry the same message for all peoples struggling for freedom from liberal-racist capitalist America. The Texas Cowboy that Negro votes helped put in the White House makes it plain to the Vietnamese and Dominicans:

We love you folks. You're just folks, just like us. Howdy, folks. We admire your struggle and aspirations for progress, your great "revolution." But now you've fallen into the hands of irresponsible Commie conspirators. We're going to honor our solemn commitments to your former masters by clobbering you with napalm bombs, vomit gas, rockets, bullets, flame throwers, and a few dirty tricks we can't mention in public. But we love you folks. After we've subdued you and lassoed you and replaced your Commie leaders with good guys of our choosing, we'll shower you with aid and surplus food and help you to your rightful place in the community of nations. Honest injun, folks.

According to Rustin and Kahn, liberals like this are our friends.

Before getting to the next point, dig that bit about nobody

being scared of Malcolm. The entire press, racist to conservative to liberal, was and is out gunning against "irresponsible" leaders, militants who are not responsible to white
liberals. Malcolm X was their worst offender. Police Com-
missioner Murphy of New York (is he one of our friends
too?) zeroed in on Malcolm X and other ghetto militants
personally. The *New York Times,* voice of the ruling class,
launched a "Blood Brothers" hoax to set the stage for doing
in Malcolm X. Just prior to the assassination, the New
York police engineered a bizarre provocation, with a police agent personally procuring dynamite in an absurd
"plot" to blow up white folks' historical monuments.

His Majesty's Uncle Tom, Carl Rowan of the U. S. Information Agency, sent Truth Teams running all over Africa,
dogging Malcolm X's tracks, trying to soften the impact
of Malcolm X's truth about Uncle Sam on our African
brothers. Even de Gaulle, who likes to stand up to Uncle
Sam and tell the old buzzard off, found Malcolm X too
dangerous to be allowed on French soil (de Gaulle is worried about the black brothers in Guadaloupe, Martinique,
"French" Guiana).

After the assassination, New York police displayed scant
interest in uncovering the conspiracy behind it. Instead they
tried to leak rumors pointing a finger at other black organizations. Unknown hands pulled off a CIA-style "Reichstag
fire" on the Black Muslim mosque in Harlem, evidently
seeking to promote fratricidal warfare among black people.

Experts Rustin and Kahn explain to us: "Malcolm's killing is . . . of a pattern stamped on ghetto life: Negroes
slashing Negroes in Harlem on a Saturday night . . ."
Just like the assassination of Patrice Lumumba???

Non-violent "love" and opposition to it is a crucial and
complex topic, and our two liberals present the usual line
that "the only alternative [to non-violent love] is passivity."
This provincial argument is a narrow view with a civil
rights protest focus, naively implying that outside the protest movement per se there is no struggle worth talking
about. While non-violence philosophy and non-violent Gan-
dhist tactics have been prominent in the Southern integration struggle, there is no evidence that this approach has
been essential (except in the sense that, if more flexible tac-

tics were brought into play, the liberals might cut off the money and thereby cripple the movement).

But it has been possible to build a mass protest movement on a non-violence basis (or despite the rigid limitations of that approach) in the rural South. This is not true for black ghettos in the North – or even in the South, as Birmingham proved. In the ghetto situation, the non-violent approach has little or no appeal to black militants or to the black masses, and even meets with hostility and disgust.

Instead of sneering, condemning, and dismissing proponents of non-violent philosophy as masochists, cowards, etc., or dismissing opposition to non-violent philosophy as loud talk by passive onlookers, etc., it would be useful to probe the question *why* non-violent philosophy appeals to many activists and *why* it repels many other activists in disgust. "Manhood" or "cowardice" have nothing to do with the matter.

Jay Jenkins, who was shot to death by cops in the Harlem "riots" of July 1964, allegedly for hurling bricks at the cops, was a hero who died with his boots on, facing the enemy. No less a hero was James Chaney, brutally mangled and murdered at the hands of fiendish Mississippians the same summer. Whatever different attitudes these two fallen brothers may have had on non-violence, white allies, integration, Negro leaders, etc., reflect differences in the history and nature of the struggle and the different problems black people face in Harlem and in rural Mississippi.

The flourishing of non-violent philosophy in the South is encouraged by attempts to win the "love" of Southern whites, or at least neutralize their obsessed overt sick racism, by the limitation of goals to civil rights and integration, and by the need to hold the "friendship" of white liberals. Cautious tactics are often dictated by the relationship of forces and the unrestrained brutish violence of Southern racists.

In big-city ghettos, on the other hand, there can be no illusion about solving problems of housing, schools, police brutality, unemployment, poverty, through reaching the hearts of whites. "Love" goes wasted, there is nobody to get non-violent with. Whites in big cities do not particularly hate Negroes, nor are they obsessed all day long with keeping each and every individual Negro in his place: "We don't hate niggers, we'd just rather not have them around," as the lady told the *Newsweek* opinion pollsters.

Picture a Harlem father trying to work the non-violent love bit on a rat about to chew up his baby's arm. "If any blood must be spilled, dear Lord, let it be the blood of my black baby, and not the blood of our rodent brothers." That approach will get him nowhere with the rats, or with the landlord, the police, his boss, or any other problem related to the society.

Since the non-violent approach fills no emotional need, is out of tune with the feelings of ghetto residents, and is obviously useless in the solution of ghetto problems, it is not only rejected but rejected with suspicion and disgust.

But rejection of Martin Luther King's peculiar version of Gandhism is not in itself a program, for North, South, or anywhere. It is only a minor prerequisite, and a negative one at that, for reaching the mass of black people and developing a meaningful and live program. Those ghetto militants who rely on blatant supermilitancy, shock tactics, and wild talk (or wild acts) are trying other futile ways of impressing whites, instead of getting down to the serious business of organizing black people and raising the political consciousness and power potential of the ghetto masses.

Malcolm X, as soon as he broke free of the Nation of Islam, addressed himself to the difficult task of getting an organization off the ground, of developing a program for the immediate struggle and a long-range program for the long haul, of soliciting and sifting through new ideas and fresh thinking, making contacts with allies abroad. Yet Rustin and Kahn, who should know better and who give the impression of being informed on things, attribute to Malcolm X the infantile posturing, obsession with violence and bombastic militancy which were alien to him.

But what else should we expect? In an interview published in the British Laborite *Tribune* last December 4, this is the way Bayard Rustin "analyzes" the psychology of ghetto dwellers who fought back against police attack in the long, hot summer of 1964:

"Rather like a child who feels he's unloved and so creates a tantrum by screaming and yelling; he is saying, essentially, 'Mother, father, I am in need of love, care and affection. I *insist* that you hear me, I *insist* that you attend to me.'"

Isn't that a damn shame! Bayard Rustin is so obsessed with the need to appeal to the "conscience" of white America, wallows so deep in morbid dependency and child-parent relationship to the liberal power structure and to Big Daddy in the White House, that he cannot help projecting his own outlook on life onto a strange people whose ways and thoughts he is incapable of comprehending or penetrating.

Among the other potshots fired by Rustin and Kahn, there is an attempt to equate Malcolm X to Booker T. Washington. "Washington was appointed the Negro leader by white philanthropists . . . Malcolm's public image was largely the creation of the white press." Our two liberals also feel a compulsion to lash out at Malcolm X's "conception of manhood and dignity," which, they find, "at least during his career with the Black Muslims – was thoroughly petit bourgeois."

These attacks are fascinating. Over and over again we hear experts and authorities (on *us*) tell it that the Muslim ideal of manhood – holding down a steady job, wearing clean, well-pressed clothes, studying and learning, keeping away from alcohol and other vices, protecting black women, etc. – is petty-bourgeois, that is middle-class.

According to these experts, if you are a family man, if you stay sober instead of getting high on cheap wine, and bring the paycheck home instead of gambling it away, you have gone stone middle-class. Is it possible to express greater contempt for working-class people in fewer words?

But how did our two liberals get into this argument? Rustin and Kahn are petty-bourgeois in social outlook, petty-bourgeois in their politics and ideology, petty-bourgeois in their livelihood, write articles in petty-bourgeois publications to a petty-bourgeois audience – there is nothing about them that is not petty-bourgeois. So eager are they to get at Malcom X's manhood that they stumble into a degrading attack on their own selves.

The same applies to the parallel with Booker T. Washington. Brother Booker T. trod the welcome mat at the

White House in his day, he was built up by the white communications media as a great and responsible Negro statesman, and was backed by white greenery. That much can be said of Negro civil rights liberals today (with the important difference that today's responsible leaders do participate in mass protests for civil rights). Here again, Rustin implicitly sneers at his own self in his eagerness to deprecate Malcolm X.

In contrast, the savage treatment of Malcolm X by the white media could hardly be called a "build-up" (except for physical murder). The organizations founded by Malcolm X subsist on nickels and dimes from the ghetto poor, not on subsidies from opulent white sugar daddies. And Big Daddy no more entertained the notion of inviting Malcolm X to see the interior furnishings of the White House than he would have thought of inviting Fidel Castro.

No finer compliment could be paid to Malcolm X.

Appendix D

Two Interviews*
By Jack Barnes

Robert Penn Warren interviewed a man named Malcolm X in June, 1964, and I helped to interview a man with the same name in January, 1965. I phrase it that way because, after reading Warren's account, I almost wondered if we had interviewed the same man. Of course, the difference was really in the interviewers, in their attitudes and assumptions.

Warren was born and raised in the South and, as a young man, believed in segregation. He has spent much of his life in the North as a writer and teacher, and is now against segregation. Stirred by the Negro upsurge, he wanted to find out more about what Negroes think. So he set out to interview many of them for his book, *Who Speaks for the Negro?* (Random House, 1965).

His approach is that of a liberal. One of his favorite questions of the people he interviewed was did they think that it would have been a good idea to have compensated the Confederate slaveholders for the slaves emancipated; he seemed to hit it off best with those who said it would have been a good idea. He evidently was smart enough to omit this question with Malcolm, or at least he doesn't mention it.

Warren goes to the Hotel Theresa in Harlem for his interview with Malcolm. "I am admitted by a strong-looking young Negro man, dressed impeccably . . . ; he is silent but watchful, smooth-faced, impassive, of ominous dignity." (Not being a poet, as is Warren, I find it hard to conceive a dignity that is "ominous.") Malcolm shakes Warren's hand, "with the slightest hint of a smile." Warren looks him over:

"The most striking thing, at first, about that face is a

---

* Reprinted from *The Militant*. February 21, 1966.

sort of stoniness, a rigidity, as though beyond all feeling. When the lips move to speak you experience a faint hint of surprise. When – as I discover later – he scores a point and the face suddenly breaks into his characteristic wide, leering, merciless smile, with the powerful even teeth gleaming beyond the very pale pink lips, the effect is, to say the least, startling. But beyond the horn-rimmed glasses always the eyes are watching, pale brown or hazel, some tint of yellow. You cannot well imagine them closed in sleep."

"After the handshake, he turns to his aide . . . . I am, for the moment, dismissed, and wander across the room, inspecting it." ". . . as he stands there across the expanse of bare, ill-swept floor, conferring with the ominous attendant . . . I am watching him, and he knows I am watching him, but he gives no sign." Malcolm's failure to give a sign that he knows Warren is watching him is clearly as sinister as the "attendant" has now become.

"Finally" Malcolm beckons Warren into the tiny room used as his office. "Malcolm X tells me that he has only a few minutes, that he has found that you waste a lot of time with reporters and then you don't get much space." And so the interview begins.

It seemed somewhat different when Barry Sheppard and I interviewed Malcolm in the same office on January 18, 1965, a month before his assassination. Our interview was taped for the *Young Socialist* (March-April, 1965; also in the pamphlet, *Malcolm X Talks to Young People,* Young Socialist Pamphlet, 1965.)

The thing that struck us first was how tired Malcolm looked. (In the *Autobiography,* Alex Haley describes the 18-hour schedule he followed.) At one point toward the end of the interview, a yawn can be heard on the tape, followed by the apology, "Excuse my tired mind." We were a little uncomfortable at first, feeling that Malcolm might need rest more urgently than we needed an interview and, because this was the first time we had met, there was some over-politeness on both sides. Malcolm sent out for coffee for the three of us, making his familiar joke about his preference for light coffee, and after that the atmosphere warmed up.

After the formal interview, we offered to type it up and bring it back, edited to fit our space requirements, for his final check and corrections. We also asked him if he would like the Young Socialist Alliance to organize a national speaking tour of campuses for him later in the year. He expressed interest in this, but did not commit himself, saying he would discuss it the next time we got together.

Let us return to poor Warren. He tries to catch Malcolm in a contradiction, but Malcolm deftly avoids the trap, and makes his own point. Warren's reaction:

"I discovered that that pale, dull yellowish face that had seemed so veiled, so stony, as though beyond all feeling, had flashed into its merciless, leering life – the sudden wolfish grin, the pale pink lips drawn hard back to show the strong teeth, the unveiled glitter of the eyes beyond the lenses, giving the sense that the lenses were only part of a clever disguise, that the eyes needed no help, that they suddenly see everything."

Malcolm had ruined his eyes reading by poor light at night while he was in prison, and says in the *Autobiography* that he had astigmatism. Never mind the facts – Warren senses "that the lenses were only part of a clever disguise" (an elaborate scheme for fooling liberals somehow). Warren didn't really need to look into Malcolm's eyes – he came to the interview convinced that Malcolm was racist, demagogic and opportunist ("He may end at the barricades, or in Congress. Or he might even end on the board of a· bank"), and that is what he went away with.

Malcolm knew the white liberal type very well, and he must have had to grin ("leer") when he saw how closely Warren was ˙conforming to the type. And when Warren asks Malcolm "if he believes in political assassination" (!), it is not hard to see why Malcolm might "turn the hard, impassive face and veiled eyes" upon Warren and say, "I wouldn't know anything about that."

I returned to Malcolm's office less than a week after our interview, bearing the edited transcript Barry had made from the tape. (If we had known this would be the last thing we would get from him, we of course would not have shortened the transcript, even slightly.) Malcolm was talking to a young man in his inner office. While I waited, for about ten minutes, one of Malcolm's co-workers, the only other person in the outer office, dozed at a reception desk.

A small stack of *Militants* lay on the desk with a couple of dimes on top.

As Malcolm read the transcript, he began to grin. When he came to the question about capitalism and the statement, "It's only a matter of time in my opinion before it will collapse completely," he said, "This is the farthest I've ever gone. They will go wild over this." I asked if he wanted to tone it down and, without hesitation, he answered no.

He said he felt the editing had sharpened up what he had originally said; that he had been tired when he gave the interview. He made very few changes and I said that would be the final copy, just as he had left it. He said, "Make any additional changes you want—it's fine. This is the kind of editing it's a pleasure to read."

Malcolm then began to talk about young revolutionaries he had met and been impressed by in Africa and Europe. He said he had a long list of them—he called them "contacts"—and would give me a copy so we could send them the issue of the *Young Socialist* that contained his interview. He also spoke about *The Militant,* and how often he had seen it abroad.

I told him I might be going to Algeria for the World Youth Festival (then scheduled for the spring of 1965) and might be able to meet some of his contacts there. He said, "Great, that would be a good experience; they have a hard time believing that revolutionaries exist in the United States." We arranged that he would give me the list after the *Young Socialist* came off the press.

I reminded him about our proposal for a national campus tour. This time he responded very favorably; he must have thought about it further and may have discussed it with some of his co-workers. He said he had learned from much experience of speaking on campus that students were in general the only whites that seemed to be open-minded. He said he was sure that the government would try to buy off the white students who were radical, that this was their main problem. He said they should "get in a closet"—away from the professors and the job offers from government and business—and think out their ideas more thoroughly and basically. They could travel the road before them in

one of two ways, he said, "–as missionaries or as revolutionaries."

He asked a lot of questions about the Young Socialist
Alliance–how many locals, where, what campuses? He
wanted to know how long the tour would last; he said he
could not make it until after his return from another trip
abroad that he was committed to make, but that would be
the best time. I said I was sure that on most campuses we
would be able to get broader sponsorship than the YSA for
his speeches, and he said he didn't care how broad or how
narrow the sponsorship would be.

He asked me if I read French and then gave me a magazine from Paris with a story about his talk there in November, 1964. He said he thought it was a communist
magazine, and that "things are very different in Europe
and Africa. There are communists and socialists all over,
and no one makes a big deal out of it. They can't imagine
how narrow-minded this country is."

Malcolm also spoke at some length about imperialism,
along what Marxists might call Luxemburgian lines–how
the West is in a real bind because the colonial revolution
is cutting off places where imperialism can expand.

I felt completely at ease with Malcolm throughout this
discussion, which lasted quite a while at his initiative. He
grew quite excited at the thought of his African youth contacts getting the *Young Socialist* interview and at the possibility of my meeting them. I had no sense of "taking" his
valuable time–he was giving it voluntarily, and not out of
mere politeness.

It is inconceivable that he would be like that with a liberal. There would be no common points of departure, no
common projects of any kind, for him to discuss with a
liberal who felt, as Warren did, that he was accomplishing
his mission when he got Malcolm to "admit" that he didn't
"see in the American system the possibility of self-regener-
ation."

Appendix E

On the First Anniversary of Malcolm X's Death*
By George Breitman

Those who arranged the assassination of Malcolm X—because they could not answer, frighten, buy or corrupt him—wanted not only to silence his voice but to prevent the consolidation of a new movement that would seriously threaten their power and privileges.

It would have been foolish a year ago, it would be foolish now, to pretend that the assassination was anything but a calamitous blow to the freedom struggle and radical movements of this country. The assassination removed the man who was best equipped to build and lead the kind of movement that will meet the immediate needs of black people and the ultimate needs of all working people. We could console ourselves by saying that his place would be filled eventually by others, because that is true, but it did not alter the fact that meanwhile our cause had suffered a crippling setback.

But we should not go to the other extreme and make the mistake of thinking that our enemies achieved everything they wanted to. Their aim was not only to kill Malcolm, but to kill his ideas. Their intention was not only to end his life, but to end his influence. They wanted him not only dead, but discredited and forgotten.

No one could be positive a year ago that they would not succeed in this second aim too. Now, after a year, I think the answer can be given with certainty—they have not succeeded. The effort to discredit him has failed, he is not forgotten, and more people have begun to understand his ideas, to understand them more accurately, than in the last year of his life. Malcolm X the man has been dead for

* A talk given at a memorial meeting sponsored by the Militant Labor Forum in New York on February 11, 1966. Reprinted from the *Young Socialist*, March-April, 1966.

a year, but the truths that he uttered and the example that he set are still marching on. With all of its power, the enemy has not been able to prevent those truths from reaching more and more people, black and white. That is what I want to demonstrate and document tonight.

Malcolm's body had still not been buried when a black lackey of the white ruling class, Carl Rowan, tried to earn some of his pay as director of the United States Misinformation Agency. Waving newspaper articles from all over the world, Rowan complained bitterly that they were misrepresenting the significance of a man who was only "an ex-convict, ex-dope peddler who became a racial fanatic." Rowan was not content to have Malcolm dead; he felt a necessity to bespatter his image and consign him to disgraceful oblivion.

That wasn't only Rowan talking, that was the government, the national government of the ruling class that was not satisfied with Malcolm dead physically, but wanted him dead morally as well. The same position was taken by the press of this ruling class. In the last pages of his *Autobiography* Malcolm had predicted that when he was dead, the press was going to smear and distort his effort to open a new road for the Negro struggle. And the *New York Times,* the outstanding big business paper in this country, fulfilled Malcolm's prediction to the hilt the very day he was assassinated, rushing into print with an editorial whose malice and bias it would be hard to match.

The *Times* editorial called Malcolm "a case history," a twisted man who turned "many true gifts to evil purpose," had a "ruthless and fanatical belief in violence," "did not seek to fit into society or into the life of his own people," saw the world in distorted fashion, and was killed by someone who came out of the "darkness that he spawned." It is probable that the authors of this editorial were so carried away by the passion of their hatred for Malcolm and what he represented that they overshot the mark and actually defeated their own purpose. But the purpose was plain – to destroy Malcolm's influence and prestige as thoroughly as the assassins' bullets had destroyed the man.

And the liberals – who preach to the ruling class, but generally accept its basic estimates and outlook – were not much better. The liberal magazine, *The Nation,* began its

March 8 editorial on the assassination with the statement, "Malcolm X was the highly intelligent, courageous leader of one segment of the Negro lunatic fringe." The lesson it drew was that the government should proceed to remove discriminatory barriers and thus prevent people from adhering to Malcolm's cause, which it called defeatist and mistaken. The editorial ended by saying that if the government would do that, then Malcolm "will in the long run have done great service not only to the Negroes but to all Americans" – even though he was the leader of a lunatic fringe, which, as any liberal knows, must be shunned and isolated.

But something has happened since those editorials were printed, something unexpected by the men who wrote them in February and March. Around the end of October, less than four months ago, two books by and about Malcolm were published – the *Autobiography* and *Malcolm X Speaks*, a collection of speeches and statements from his last year – and these became the means for registering what had happened to Malcolm's reputation and standing during the seven or eight months after his death.

You have heard what the editors of the *Times* said and wanted people to believe in February. But on November 5 they printed a review of the *Autobiography* by a member of their staff, and lo and behold, it's not along quite the same lines as their February 22 editorial. The reviewer is Eliot Fremont-Smith, and he begins as follows:

"It is probably fair to say that the majority of the public regards Malcolm X . . . as a violence-preaching 'Black Muslim' racial agitator who reaped his own bloody end." He then adds, and this is what is new (for the *Times*), "There is, however, another view of Malcolm X – one that is increasingly prevalent among civil rights advocates – that with his death American Negroes lost their most able, articulate and compelling spokesman." Fremont-Smith doesn't take sides in favor of this increasingly prevalent view and against the view fostered by his bosses – he says only, "Both views represent parts of the truth." But now at least the so-called part of the truth that was completely absent from the February editorial is getting a certain amount of airing and hearing.

Fremont-Smith notes now "that in the last year of his

life he radically modified certain of his ideas and began
to take an active role in the securing of Negro rights within, not apart from, American society." He continues: "How
important a spokesman he could have been for American
Negroes had he lived remains in doubt." At any rate, this
raises a doubt about the position of the *Times* editors, who
showed no doubts whatever. Fremont-Smith casts further
doubts on their position when he says, "As this extraordinary autobiography shows, the source of Malcolm X's
power was not alone in his intelligence, energy, electric
personality or ability to grow and change, remarkable as
these were. Its source was that he understood, perhaps
more profoundly than any other Negro leader, the full,
shocking extent of America's psychological destruction of
its Negroes" (which he calls "an almost automatic function
of white society").

The point I am trying to make is that the authors of that
scurrilous *Times* editorial in February could not have
foreseen that in November they would have to print an
article so much at variance with their own prejudices. This
was not because the *Times* editors have changed, have
reformed, have become more honest – but because the atmosphere has changed. They simply could not get away
in November with the kind of falsification they thought
possible in February. Too many people are learning the
truth, and the editors have been forced to readjust a little.

The editors of *The Nation* suffered a similar fate. In
March they had belittled Malcolm as the leader of a lunatic
fringe, but on November 8 they printed a review of the
Autobiography by Truman Nelson which began by saying,
"This is the story of a man struck down on his way to
becoming a revolutionary and a liberator of his people."
Nothing about lunatic fringes. And near the end Nelson
says of Malcolm, after his final return from Africa in the
autumn of 1964, "I heard him in Harlem, on a platform
with Babu, the Zanzibar revolutionary, say the problem
is now simply the oppressed against the oppressor. He
had begun to renew himself, and his regenerated purpose
began to take form, a political form. He was talking now
like a member of the revolutionary majority." Talking like
a member of the revolutionary majority probably strikes

some of *The Nation* editors as lunatic stuff too, but they're not saying that now.

Earlier, in the September 20 *Nation*, Harvey Swados, writing about the radical parties in this country, expressed the conviction that "Malcolm did have a remarkable capacity for political growth," which, he said, "many white liberals refused to recognize, perhaps because it is a capacity that is foreign to them."

This is true – most white liberals lack that capacity. So do black liberals, even black liberals who call themselves radicals or social-democrats, like Bayard Rustin. But even in Rustin we have witnessed a certain change during the months we have been examining, a change which can be explained only by a change in the prevailing intellectual atmosphere. Rustin and Malcolm were political opponents, because Rustin favors sidetracking the Negro struggle into the Democratic Party and uses the most radical-sounding arguments to justify this policy, while Malcolm called this policy what it is – political Uncle Tomism. Immediately after the assassination, Rustin and Tom Kahn did a hatchet job on Malcolm, printed in *Dissent* and *New America* – an article designed to cut Malcolm down so that no young militant would ever look in his direction for guidance or inspiration. After the *Autobiography* appeared, however, Rustin reviewed it in the November 14 *Book Week*. Now Rustin too had to sing a slightly different tune, had to show a little more respect for Malcolm the man, even though he continued to belittle his achievement and confuse his evolution by garbling together Malcolm's positions on important questions from different and conflicting periods of his life.

Having a capacity for growth that is lacking among most liberals, some radicals have been able to learn things in the year since Malcolm's death. An example is Emile Capouya, who reviewed Malcolm's *Autobiography* and a book by Elijah Muhammad in the *Saturday Review* of November 20. I think it is worth quoting because Capouya is both honest and independent. Capouya discusses his attitude to Malcolm during his lifetime, which he supposes represents the majority opinion still:

"As long as he was a follower of Elijah Muhammad, I was repelled by what I knew of his economic and social program, his irreconcilable attitude toward the whites, the puritanism of the Nation of Islam's moral doctrines, and the bad grammar of the sect's newspaper, *Muhammad Speaks*. The Black Muslim demand for a separate state within the United States I regarded as a piece of cynical demagoguery, or perhaps plain foolishness. What it came down to is that Malcolm X was talking revolution, his own variety, and since that was not the same as mine, I could fall back on all the familiar excuses for not using my imagination. When Malcolm X parted company with Elijah Muhammad, made his pilgrimage to Mecca, returned bearing a more conciliatory racial message, and began to involve himself in direct political activity, I grew slightly more sympathetic.

"Now that he is dead, and the social forces to which he gave expression are for the moment thwarted, I can see how badly I misjudged the man and the movement. It has taken me a long time, but I begin to see why many Negro intellectuals, and radicals black and white, were so impressed by him, applauded his intransigence while he was alive, and felt personally diminished by his death. Right now, in this country, every man stands between the devil and the deep blue sea. The ideals we profess as a people have scarcely any other function than to color greed at home and violence abroad. We are in a moral and political crisis. Almost alone, Malcolm X knew it and declared it; his doctrine was cast in terms of race, but that was very nearly an accident." (Elsewhere in the review Capouya makes the correct point that *class* questions are often expressed in *racial* terms.)

Much the same thing that happened to Emile Capouya has been happening to other people, especially student rebels. Donald Stanley, reviewing the *Autobiography* in the October 14 *San Francisco Examiner,* writes:

". . . one of the really surprising things that's happening is the spreading legend of the late 'Black Muslim' leader whose influence has failed to stop at graveside.

"Malcolm's ghost is walking today alongside not only the blacks engaged in their fight for rights and equality, but it insinuates itself more and more frequently into such nonracial student movements as those which animate Berkeley."

Most of the changed opinions about Malcolm that I have been reporting up to now have been by white people, not black. That is because there has been little or no change in black people's opinions. Without hearing everything Malcolm said, without knowing whether he had altered his views on this or that question, the masses of black people sensed, felt and knew that he was speaking for them all the time and to them most of the time. They knew that unlike most Negro leaders, he could not be bought. Foolish white liberals like Robert Penn Warren could say, in his book *Who Speaks for the Negro?*, that Malcolm "may end at the barricades, or in Congress. Or he might even end on the board of a bank." But the black masses knew, before the assassination, that Malcolm would never sell out, and the assassination only confirmed this conviction. Middle class Negro leaders, the moderates and liberals, are keenly aware of what the masses think about Malcolm. That is why, despite their hostility toward almost everything he represented, they have been careful about the way they speak and write about him — more careful, for example, than Bayard Rustin or Carl Rowan, whose main audience is not the Negro masses.

When we examine Malcolm's standing in the black community we come to something apparently paradoxical. Malcolm was a black nationalist; in the first months after he left the Black Muslims he was a pure-and-simple black nationalist, and in his final months he was something more than that, he was a black nationalist plus social revolutionist (although he had then begun to have doubts about the black nationalist label).

Now black nationalism — this doctrine or ideology or tendency with which the name of Malcolm was and is associated — had reached the height of its popularity in the black community from 1962 until around the middle of 1964. Many more people called themselves black nationalists during that period than ever before. Black nationalists were self-confident in those years, they felt the wind was in their sails. But around the middle of 1964 something happened that changed this situation. I think it was the nomination of Goldwater, which precipitated a crisis, a political dilemma, in black nationalist circles. I cannot go into that here, but I think I could show that whatever the reason was, a change did begin to take place then among most of the people who considered themselves black nationalists. Some of the steam began to go out of them, some of them stopped calling themselves black nationalists, confusion set in, morale fell. This was noticeably the case after the assassination of Malcolm, the man so many people had counted on to lead in the formation of a new, nationwide black nationalist movement.

And yet—and this is the paradoxical part—while *organizationally* the black nationalist tendency has suffered serious setbacks in the last year or two, *ideologically* its influence has spread far, wide and deep. It is as though it was locked out of the door and came creeping in the window. For today many of the ideas, demands and slogans originated by black nationalists in 1962, '63 and '64—ideas, demands and slogans associated in the public mind above all with Malcolm X—are common coin in most of the black community and even in many of the civil rights organizations that didn't want to touch Malcolm with a ten-foot pole.

Malcolm is dead and the movement he wanted to build has not grown or prospered organizationally. But many of their ideas—black leadership, black power, building a base in the ghetto, control of the ghetto, self-defense, racial pride and solidarity, identification with the colonial revolution and Africa, independent black political action—these and other concepts, which were considered the unique attributes of black nationalism and Malcolm X two years ago, are now generally accepted in the black community, or they are not argued about, or at the very least they are given lip service even by civil rights organizations that repudiated and denounced them not long ago.

The continued spread of Malcolm's ideas can be illustrated by two of the major developments of the last year— Watts and the movement against the war in Vietnam.

Malcolm predicted Watts, and probably would have been blamed for it if he had lived. He predicted that 1965 would see the biggest explosion yet, and Watts was certainly the biggest and most explosive demonstration against racial oppression of our time. Malcolm did not call such explosions "race riots"—he used the word "pogrom" to describe the Harlem events of 1964—and he would have concurred with the youth of Watts who called their uprising a revolt, not a riot. Even the most obtuse commentators on the Watts events were compelled to recognize the basically black nationalist and potentially revolutionary character of the Watts uprising, which is only another way of saying its Malcolmite character. In the 1964 struggle, the people of Harlem who booed Bayard Rustin and James Farmer shouted, "We want Malcolm." They could not do that in Watts in 1965. But in essence the people of Watts were shouting, through their actions, for a leadership with the integrity and intransigence of Malcolm.

Malcolm died just around the time of the first major escalation of the counter-revolutionary war against the people of Vietnam, and only eight weeks before the April March on Washington where the present antiwar movement was born. But he had been speaking out against the United States government's war from the beginning. He spoke out against it long before Martin Luther King, and without any equivocation about where his sympathies lay. He spoke out against it in the spirit of the best and strongest parts of last month's antiwar statement by SNCC, and would surely have supported the antiwar demonstrations scheduled to take place in the South this weekend. William Worthy reported in the November 20 *National Guardian* that during the International Days of Protest rally in Berkeley on October 16, one speaker on the sound truck remarked to another: "Has it occurred to you that if Malcolm X had not been assassinated last February, he would undoubtedly be speaking here today or at one of the other big demonstrations? His presence would have added an important extra dimension to the protest." He could also have said, with equal accuracy, that Malcolm was one of the influences that had helped to educate and inspire many of the thousands of young people who came out into the streets that day. Malcolm placed his greatest hopes in young people, in students; he would have felt his hopes were being confirmed by the rise of the present antiwar movement, and he would have reached out the hand of solidarity toward it.

In the Summer issue of *Dissent*, the social-democratic magazine which some people are beginning to call *Assent*, Irving Howe, its editor, claimed that he had heard Mal-

colm say at a meeting "that he would go, not unarmed,
to Mississippi, *if* the Negroes there would ask him to come:
a condition that could only leave him safely North, since
the last thing the Negroes of Mississippi needed or wanted
was Malcolm's military aid." Since this was a misrepre-
sentation both of what Malcolm had said and of sentiment
in the South, I wrote *Dissent* a letter pointing out that
Malcolm did not remain "safely" North, but went to Alabama and spoke there twice in the last month of his life,
getting an enthusiastic reception from the Selma students,
and was scheduled to speak in Mississippi the weekend he
was killed. And I added that "the spread of the Deacons
for Defense and Justice into Mississippi indicates that Howe
is not speaking for all Mississippi's Negroes" when he says
they don't need or want Malcolm's position on self-defense.
Howe replied in the Autumn issue that he would not argue
about what Malcolm had said, but insisted that it would
not do "to invoke the Deacons" as an example of what
Malcolm was advocating. "For that group, whatever judgment one may make of its methods, is involved with, part
of the Civil Rights Movement; it works together with CORE;
it does not, as Malcolm did, talk violence and practice
abstentionism."

Now the question is not whether Malcolm was willing to
work together with CORE on certain projects; of course he
was willing—they were the ones who were unwilling. The
question is: Are the Deacons the kind of self-defense movement Malcolm advocated, or aren't they? I think the answer is that they are, that Howe is trying to create a distinction that doesn't exist in reality, as part of his tendency's
persistent effort to cut Malcolm down. But if anyone doesn't
agree, I would offer the testimony of the Deacons themselves. In particular, I would offer the testimony of Henry
Austan, a young man who joined the Deacons in Bogalusa last year, around the same time Malcolm was killed.
Austan is out on bond and faces trial, with a possible
ten-year prison sentence, for shooting a racist assailant in
self-defense during a civil rights march in Bogalusa last
July. Here are some of the things Henry Austan said, as
reported in the November 22 *Militant:*

"The Deacons have given the Negro throughout the nation an organization they can point to with dignity. There

is no dignity in the non-violent march . . . There is no dignity when a Negro woman is attacked . . . The attackers have no respect for the non-violent. . . .

"They patted Dr. King on the head when he used non-violence in Alabama. If non-violence is such a good thing, why don't we have a non-violent army in Vietnam? When King condemned the Deacons for using 'violence' in defending Negroes' lives and property, they gave him a Nobel prize. When Dr. King condemned me for shooting a white racist, they called him a responsible leader. When King condemned the U. S. for armed intervention in Vietnam, they said Dr. King had stopped being responsible and had gone into meddling.

"If violence is right in Vietnam, then surely violence is right in Mississippi. If violence can be a righteous tool for the white man, then surely it can be just as righteous for the black man. If violence can be used to murder defenseless women and children in Vietnam, then certainly it can be used in Louisiana to defend Negroes' lives and property.

"It seems funny to me they want me to fight the Vietcong, when the Vietcong never called me a nigger."

Whose voice does that resemble, if not Malcolm's?—even though it comes from a young man who didn't become active until Malcolm was dead. So it is not at all surprising to hear Henry Austan continue in that *Militant* interview and say:

"Malcolm X is my idol. Malcolm had not yet reached his peak, but I believe he was on the right road. The road I'm on is the one I think he was on. I think he believed that the black man in America had to unite and to stand up. I think this is what he was trying to do—unite the Negroes. He once said, 'Freedom by any means necessary'—which I made my motto. I hope it will become the motto of the entire black mass of this country."

So Malcolm's ideas have been spreading since his death, in the South as well as the North—not only his ideas on the specific question of self-defense, but his whole outlook, which was summed up in the motto the Henry Austans have chosen and hope will become the motto of all black people in this country. They are taking root and spreading, especially among the young people—those in their twenties

and late teens, and younger even than that. I want to con-
clude my documentation by citing a recent incident as encouraging in its way as Henry Austan's remarks and example.

There is a Saturday afternoon TV program in New York
called "Speak Out" which is conducted by Sonny Fox over
station WNEW-TV. Sarah Slack reported in the November
20 *Amsterdam News* that forty high school students were
on that program discussing the questions, "Who are your
heroes?" and "Why are they your heroes?" The expected
answers were indicated by a row of blown-up photographs
they had on display–pictures of John F. Kennedy, John
Glenn, John Wayne, Lyndon Johnson and others of that
type. To the probable surprise of the authorities, one student, described in the article as "a clean-cut American teen-
age Negro boy," said:

"Malcolm X, more than any other individual, helped the
Negro race raise the image of itself. And he, more than
any other, helped the Negro show more pride in being a
Negro."

Another youth, white, said: "Malcolm X is a hero to me
because he stood up like a man and fought so strongly
for his beliefs. Malcolm X did not run over anybody to
get him to believe as he did. He simply talked and those
who want to believe him did so."

And a young girl, also white, said: "Malcolm X fought
for what he believed in. It is right for a person to fight
for his beliefs."

I am not sure about the accuracy of the saying about
what comes out of the mouths of babes, but I do believe
that what comes out of the mouths of teenagers is significant. For they are the next generation, the one just around
the corner, who will be heard before the 1960s have ended.
And when the truth has taken root among people still in
junior high and high school, when they have been able to
pierce through the anti-Malcolm propaganda and brain-
washing and to identify with him, black and white, then
I think we have every reason to believe that the propagandists and brainwashers of the ruling class have failed, and
that Malcolm's place in history will be as high and hon-
orable as his influence on the next revolutionary generation
will be strong and productive.

NOTES

Chapter 1: The Split

1. Robert Vernon, "Malcolm X: Voice of the Black Ghetto," *International Socialist Review*, Spring, 1965.

2. Malcolm X, *Malcolm X Speaks*, Selected Speeches and Statements, edited with prefatory notes by George Breitman, New York, Merit Publishers, 1965, p. 70.

3. David Herman, "Malcolm X Assails U.S. Role in Congo," *The Militant*, Dec. 7, 1964.

4. Malcolm X (with the assistance of Alex Haley), *The Autobiography of Malcolm X*. introduction by M.S. Handler, epilogue by Alex Haley, New York, Grove Press, 1965, p. 398.

5. *Ibid.*, pp. 290-291.

6. *Ibid.*, p. 293.

7. M.S. Handler, "Malcolm's Plans Irk Muslims," *New York Times*, Nov. 8, 1964.

8. Malcolm X, *Autobiography*, p. 200.

9. *New York Times*, "Malcolm X Scores U.S. and Kennedy," Dec. 2, 1963.

10. Malcolm X, *Autobiography*, pp. 305-309.

11. *Extra*, a 32-page tabloid newspaper devoted entirely to the Los Angeles case, undated.

12. Malcolm X, *Autobiography*, pp. 293-294.

13. Louis E. Lomax, *When the Word Is Given. . .* , Cleveland, World Publishing Co., 1963, p. 179.

14. M.S. Handler, "Malcolm X Splits with Muhammad," *New York Times*, March 9, 1964.

Chapter 2: The Transition Period

1. Question and answer period, Militant Labor Forum, New York, April 8, 1964.

2. Malcolm X, *Autobiography*, pp. 279-280.

3. *Malcolm X Speaks*, p. 213.

4. Marlene Nadle, "Malcolm X: The Complexity of a Man in the Jungle," *Village Voice*, Feb. 25, 1965.

5. Frank Kofsky, "Malcolm X," *Monthly Review*, Sept., 1966.

Chapter 3: Radicalism

1. Malcolm X, *Autobiography*, p. 372.
2. *Ibid.*, p. 381.
3. *Ibid.*, p. 424.
4. *Ibid.*, p. xvi.
5. William Worthy, "Malcolm X Says Group Will Stress Politics," *National Guardian,* March 21, 1964.
6. A. B. Spellman, "Interview with Malcolm X," *Monthly Review,* May, 1964.
7. Carlos E. Russell, "Exclusive Interview with Brother Malcolm X," *Liberator,* May, 1964.
8. *Malcolm X Speaks.* pp. 45-57.
9. James Farmer, *Freedom—When?* New York, Random House, 1966, p. 96.
10. Truman Nelson, "Delinquent's Progress," *The Nation,* Nov. 8, 1965.
11. *Malcolm X Speaks,* p. 71.
12. *Ibid.*, p. 223.
13. *Ibid.*, p. 215.
14. *Ibid.*, p. 65.
15. *Ibid.*, p. 69.
16. *Ibid.*
17. *Saturday Evening Post,* "I'm Talking to You, White Man," Sept. 12, 1964.
18. A letter to the author, April 4, 1965.
19. *Malcolm X Speaks.* pp. 128-130.
20. *Ibid.*, p. 153.
21. *Ibid.*, p. 155.
22. *Ibid.*, pp. 219-220.
23. *Ibid.*, p. 215.
24. *Ibid.*, pp. 45-57.
25. *Ibid.*, p. 232.
26. *Ibid.*, p. 233.

Chapter 4: Allies and Alliances

1. *Malcolm X Speaks,* p. 52.
2. *Ibid.*
3. *Monthly Review,* June, 1965.
4. *Malcolm X Speaks,* p. 98.
5. *Ibid.*, p. 5.
6. *Ibid.*, pp. 236-237.
7. *Ibid.*, pp. 21-22.
8. Spellman, *Monthly Review,* May, 1964.
9. *Malcolm X Speaks,* p. 70.
10. *Ibid.*
11. *Ibid.*, pp. 222-223.
12. Nadle, *Village Voice,* Feb. 25, 1965.

Chapter 5: Separatism and Black Nationalism

1. Malcolm X, *Autobiography,* p. 275.
2. Farmer, *Freedom – When?,* p. 112.
3. William A. Price, "Negro Marchers Ask 'Black Power,'" *National Guardian,* June 25, 1966.
4. M. S. Handler, "Farmer Says Mood of Negroes Is One of Growing Militancy," *New York Times,* Feb. 10, 1966.
5. C. Eric Lincoln, *My Face Is Black,* Boston, Beacon Press, 1964.
6. Malcolm X, "God's Judgment of White America," Dec. 1, 1963, New York, manuscript of unpublished speech.
7. Malcolm X in symposium on "Contact" program on radio station WINS, New York, Feb. 18, 1965.
8. *Malcolm X Speaks,* p. 10.
9. *Ibid.,* pp. 20-21.
10. Spellman, *Monthly Review,* May, 1964.
11. *Ibid.*
12. *Malcolm X Speaks,* p. 38.
13. *Ibid.,* p. 51.
14. *Freedom Now: A New Stage in the Struggle for Black Emancipation,* New York, Pioneer Publishers, 1963.
15. Question and answer period, Militant Labor Forum, New York, April 8, 1964.
16. David Herman, "Malcolm X Back from Africa – Urges Black United Front," *The Militant,* June 1, 1964.
17. *Malcolm X Speaks,* pp. 226-227.
18. *Ibid.,* p. 213.
19. *Ibid.,* p. 217.
20. *Ibid.,* pp. 228-229.
21. George Breitman, Harold Cruse and Clifton DeBerry, *Marxism and the Negro Struggle,* New York, Pioneer Publishers, 1965.
22. Malcolm X in symposium on "The Crisis of Racism," sponsored by the Committee to Aid the Monroe Defendants, New York, May 1, 1962, tape-recorded by radio station WBAI-FM.

Chapter 6: Organization

1. Farmer, *Freedom – When?,* p. 101.
2. Milton Henry, "New Glory Visits Malcolm X," *Now!* (Detroit), March-April, 1966.
3. Farmer, *Freedom – When?,* pp. 94-95.
4. *Malcolm X Speaks,* p. 21.
5. *Ibid.,* p. 38.
6. Russell, *Liberator,* May, 1964.
7. *Malcolm X Speaks,* pp. 40-41.
8. *Malcolm X Talks to Young People,* New York, Young Socialist Pamphlet, October, 1965, p. 27.
9. Nadle, *Village Voice,* Feb. 25, 1965.

Chapter 7: Malcolm and His Critics

1. Irving Howe, *Dissent,* Autumn, 1965.
2. Farmer, *Freedom – When?,* p. 99.
3. Bayard Rustin, "Race Tension in the Ghetto Unites Integrationists and Black Muslims," *New America,* Sept. 22, 1961.
4. Saul Friedman, "Rights Parley Scorned," *Detroit Free Press,* June 2, 1966.
5. Earl Caldwell and Robert Terrell, "The Words Stir a Debate Here," *New York Post,* July 6, 1966.
6. David Llorens, "Books Noted," *Negro Digest,* May, 1966.
7. Phonograph record "Malcolm X Speaks Again," Twenty Grand Records, New York, 1965.
8. Irving Howe, "New Styles in 'Leftism,'" *Dissent,* Summer, 1965.

RELATED READING

Books

Baldwin, James. *The Fire Next Time.* New York: Dial Press, 1963.

Bennett, Lerone, Jr. *The Negro Mood.* Chicago: Johnson Publishing Co., 1964. (Malcolm recommended its chapter on "The Black Establishment.")

——. *Confrontation: Black and White.* Chicago: Johnson Publishing Co., 1965.

Bontemps, Arna and Conroy, Jack. *Anyplace But Here.* New York: Hill and Wang, 1966. (Contains a chapter on the Black Muslims and Malcolm.)

Broderick, Francis L. and Meier, August (eds.). *Negro Protest Thought in the Twentieth Century.* New York: Bobbs-Merrill Co., 1966. (Contains "Separation or Integration: A Debate" between Malcolm X and James Farmer, reprinted from *Dialogue Magazine,* May, 1962.)

Clark, Kenneth B. (ed.) *The Negro Protest: James Baldwin, Malcolm X, Martin Luther King Talk with Kenneth B. Clark.* Boston: Beacon Press, 1963.

Essien-Udom, E. U. *Black Nationalism: A Search for an Identity in America.* Chicago: University of Chicago Press, 1962. (A Nigerian scholar's study of the Black Muslims.)

Farmer, James. *Freedom – When?* New York: Random House, 1966. (Contains a chapter on black nationalism and Malcolm.)

Hernton, Calvin C. *White Papers for White Americans.* New York: Doubleday & Co., 1966. (Contains a chapter on Malcolm as an "existential Negro.")

Jones, LeRoi. *Home: Social Essays.* New York: William Morrow & Co., 1966. (Contains a chapter entitled "The Legacy of Malcolm X, and the Coming of the Black Nation.")

Lincoln, C. Eric. *The Black Muslims in America.* Boston: Beacon Press, 1961.

——. *My Face Is Black.* Boston: Beacon Press, 1964. (Contains discussion of Malcolm's prospects after the split.)

Lomax, Louis E. *The Negro Revolt.* New York: Harper & Row, 1962.

———. *When the Word Is Given* . . . Cleveland: World Publishing Co., 1963. (Contains several of Malcolm's speeches, 1960-3, useful for contrast with those from his last year.)

Malcolm X (with the assistance of Alex Haley). *The Autobiography of Malcolm X,* introduction by M. S. Handler, epilogue by Alex Haley, New York: Grove Press, 1965.

———. *Malcolm X Speaks,* Selected Speeches and Statements, edited with prefatory notes by George Breitman, New York: Merit Publishers, 1965.

Warren, Robert Penn. *Who Speaks for the Negro?,* New York: Random House, 1965. (Contains a report of an interview with Malcolm in June, 1964.)

Pamphlets

Breitman, George (ed.). *Documents on the Negro Struggle.* New York: Pioneer Publishers (Bulletin of Marxist Studies, Number 4), 1962. (Contains the texts of discussions with Leon Trotsky about "self-determination" and the American Negro, 1933 and 1939.)

———. *Malcolm X: The Man and His Ideas.* New York: Pioneer Publishers, March, 1965. (The text of a memorial speech given in Detroit on March 5, 1965.)

———, Cruse, Harold, and DeBerry, Clifton. *Marxism and the Negro Struggle.* New York: Pioneer Publishers, March, 1965.

Malcolm X. *Two Speeches by Malcolm X.* New York: Pioneer Publishers, March, 1965. (Contains speeches at Militant Labor Forum in New York on April 8, 1964, and January 7, 1965; excerpts from Militant Labor Forum symposium on May 29, 1964; text of interview by Harry Ring over New York station WBAI-FM on January 28, 1965.)

———. *Malcolm X Talks to Young People.* New York: Young Socialist Pamphlet, October, 1965. (Contains excerpts from talk to youth from McComb, Mississippi, on December 31, 1964; interview by *Young Socialist* on January 18, 1965; excerpts from a report about Malcolm's impact on Africa by SNCC leaders John Lewis and Donald Harris, dated December 14, 1964.)

Mitchell, Sara. *Brother Malcolm.* New York: Malcolm X Memorial Committee, May, 1965. (Prepared for a meeting commemorating Malcolm's 40th birthday.)

Socialist Party. *To Build a Better World: The 1962 Socialist Platform.* New York: Socialist Party, 1962. (Contains a section against black nationalism.)

Socialist Workers Party. *Freedom Now: A New Stage in the Struggle for Negro Emancipation.* New York: Pioneer Publishers, October, 1963. (This resolution, adopted by a convention in July, 1963, contains a Marxist discussion of black nationalism and separatism.)

Vernon, Robert. *The Black Ghetto.* New York: Pioneer Publishers, October, 1964. (This collection of articles from *The Militant* discusses the significance of a Black Muslim rally, the Harlem rent strike, the 1964 uprising in Harlem, and "Wechsler's Attack on Malcolm X.")

Periodicals

Adams, Alvin. "Malcolm X 'Seemed Sincere' About Helping Cause: Mrs. King." *Jet,* March 11, 1965. (About Malcolm's speech to students in Selma, Alabama, in February, 1965, while Martin Luther King was in jail.)

Allen, Robert. "Malcolm X: 2/21/65." *Village Voice,* February 17, 1966. (Eyewitness account of the assassination.)

Berger, Morroe. "The Black Muslims." *Horizon,* Winter, 1964.

Black, Pearl. "Malcolm X Returns." *Liberator,* January, 1965. (Report of the first OAAU rally held after Malcolm's second return from Africa, on November 29, 1964.)

Bone, Robert. "A Black Man's Quarrel With the Christian God." *New York Times* Book Review, September 11, 1966.

Braden, Anne. "The SNCC Trends: Challenge to White America." *The Southern Patriot,* May, 1966.

Bradley, Edward. (as told to Louis E. Lomax) "Malcolm Escaped Killers in Los Angeles by James Bond-Type Ruse." *Paterson Morning Call,* February 25, 1965.

Breitman, George. "New Force Can Bring Major Rights Gains" and "His Stand Can Unite and Build Movement." *The Militant,* March 30 and April 6, 1964. (A two-part series appraising the split.)

——. "Going to the UN Can Help, But It's No Cure-All." *The Militant,* May 25, 1964. (Malcolm sent the author his appreciation for this critical article.)

——. "Malcolm X's Murder and the N.Y. Police," "More Questions on Malcolm X's Murder," and "Why Isn't Daily Press Interested in Who Killed Malcolm X?" *The Militant,* July 12, August 9 and August 23, 1965. (A three-part series raising questions about the assassination.)

Capouya, Emile. "A Brief Return from Mecca." *Saturday Review,* November 20, 1965. (An intellectual's report of how his opinion of Malcolm changed.)

Chevigny, Bell Gale. "Malcolm X's Autobiography." *Village Voice*, March 3, 1966.

Clarke, John Henrik. "The Man and His Mission." *Freedomways*, Winter, 1966.

Cleage, Albert B., Jr. "The Next Step: An Analysis of the Black Revolution." *The Illustrated News* (Detroit), May 4, 1964. (A defense of black nationalism by the then state chairman of the Freedom Now Party of Michigan.)

Cleaver, Eldridge. "Letters from Prison." *Ramparts*, August, 1966. (A California prisoner, who had gone "with the Malcolm faction" after the split, reports how the news of the assassination was received in his prison.)

Cruse, Harold W. "Revolutionary Nationalism and the Afro-American." *Studies on the Left*, Vol. II, No. 3, 1962. (Discussion of this article by Richard Greenleaf and Clark H. Foreman, with replies by Cruse, in *Studies on the Left*, Vol. III, No. 1, 1962.)

Danzig, David. "The Meaning of Negro Strategy." *Commentary*, February, 1964.

Diamond, Stanley. "The Apostate Muslim." *Dissent*, Spring, 1965.

Domrese, Robert J. "A Struggle with the Wrong Image." *Harvard Crimson*, May 24, 1966.

Dunayevskaya, Raya. "Malcolm X and 'Old Radicals.'" *News and Letters* (Detroit), April, 1964.

Fremont-Smith, Eliot. "An Eloquent Testament." *New York Times*, November 5, 1965.

Friedman, Murray. "The White Liberal's Retreat." *Atlantic Monthly*, January, 1963.

Gardner, Jigs. "The Murder of Malcolm X." *Monthly Review*, April, 1965.

Glazer, Nathan. "Negroes and Jews: The New Challenge to Pluralism." *Commentary*, December, 1964.

Hall, Gordon D. "Malcolm X: The Man and the Myth." *Boston Sunday Herald*, February 28, 1965.

Handler, M. S. "Malcolm X Splits With Muhammad." *New York Times*, March 9, 1964.

Henry, Laurence. "Malcolm X Lives." *Cavalier*, June, 1966.

Henry, Milton. "New Glory Visits Malcolm X." *Now!*, March-April, 1966.

Hentoff, Nat. "Elijah in the Wilderness," *The Reporter*, August 4, 1960.

Herman, David. "3,000 Cheer Malcolm X At Opening Rally in Harlem." *The Militant*, March 30, 1964.

—-. "Malcolm X Details Black Nationalist Views." *The Militant*, April 20, 1964.

----. "Malcolm X Back from Africa – Urges Black United Front," *The Militant,* June 1, 1964.

----. "Malcolm X Launches a New Organization." *The Militant,* July 13, 1964.

----. "Malcolm X Assails U. S. Role in Congo." *The Militant,* December 7, 1964.

----. "Malcolm X Discusses Bombing of Home." *The Militant,* February 22, 1965.

----. "Malcolm X's Last Meeting." *The Militant,* March 1, 1965. (A representative selection of reports about Malcolm's public rallies in New York during his last year.)

Holt, Len. "Malcolm X The Mirror." *Liberator,* February, 1966.

Howe, Irving. "New Styles in 'Leftism.'" *Dissent,* Summer, 1965. (Contains a section on black nationalism and Malcolm.)

Hunt, Frank. "Malcolm X Still Lives." *Baltimore Afro-American,* February 19, 1966.

Illo, John. "The Rhetoric of Malcolm X." *Columbia University Forum,* Spring, 1966.

Jackson, James E. "A Fighting People Forging New Unity." *The Worker,* July 7, 1963. (A strong denunciation by *The Worker's* editor of the Black Muslims, Malcolm, Robert F. Williams and *Liberator.* Also appears in the theoretical organ of the Communist Party, U. S. A., *Political Affairs,* August, 1963, under the title, "A Fighting People Forging Unity.")

Jones, Theodore. "Malcolm X Knew He Was a 'Marked Man.'" *New York Times,* February 22, 1965. (About an interview three days before the assassination.)

Kahn, Tom. See Rustin, Bayard.

Kempton, Murray. "The Fruit of Islam." *New York World-Telegram and Sun,* February 23, 1965.

King, Martin Luther, Jr. "The Nightmare of Violence." *New York Amsterdam News,* March 13, 1965.

Kirk, Russell. "Malcolm X's Promise Was Murdered Too." *Detroit Free Press,* March 2, 1965.

Kirsch, Robert R. "The Real and Imagined Faces of Malcolm X." *Los Angeles Times,* November 5, 1965.

Kofsky, Frank. "Blues People." *Review I, Monthly Review* Supplement, 1965.

----. "Black Revolution in Music." *Liberator,* February, 1966. (A letter about Marxism and "soul," with a reply by Lawrence P. Neal.)

----. "Malcolm X." *Monthly Review,* September, 1966.

Larner, Jeremy. "McComb vs. Harlem." *Dissent,* Spring, 1965. (A report about the visit of young people from McComb, Mississippi, to New York during the Christmas holiday, 1964. This includes an account of what Malcolm told them that is refuted by the tape recording of what Malcolm actually said.)

Lane, Ann J. "Will the Word Be Given?" *Studies on the Left,* Summer, 1964.

Leiman, Melvin. "Malcolm X." *Liberation,* April, 1965.

Lerner, Max. "Malcolm X and 'White Devils.'" *Detroit News,* March 16, 1964.

——. "Malcolm's Death." *New York Post,* February 26, 1965.

Lightfoot, Claude. "Negro Nationalism and the Black Muslims." *Political Affairs,* July, 1962. (This appraisal by a leading spokesman of the Communist Party was based on a lecture given in Chicago.)

Lincoln, C. Eric. "The Meaning of Malcolm X." *Christian Century,* April 7, 1965.

Llorens, David, "Books Noted" (*Malcolm X Speaks*). *Negro Digest,* May, 1966.

Lomax, Almena. "Notes on a Nationalist's Death." *The Tribune* (Los Angeles), March 15, 1965.

Lubell, Samuel. "Did Malcolm's Ironic Role Advance Rights?" *Detroit Free Press,* March 1, 1965.

Malcolm X. "We Are All Blood Brothers." *Liberator,* July, 1964. (Comments on his first trip abroad in 1964.)

——. "Racism: The Cancer That Is Destroying America." *Egyptian Gazette* (Cairo), August 25, 1964.

——. "The Black Struggle in the United States." *Présence Africaine,* English edition, No. 2, 1965. (The text of Malcolm's talk in Paris on November 23, 1964, with answers to 24 questions from the floor.)

Mandel, Bernard. "The Freedom Struggle: Revolt to Revolution." *International Socialist Review,* Spring, 1964.

Massaquoi, Hans. "Mystery of Malcolm X." *Ebony,* September, 1964.

McGill, Ralph. "Essay on Malcolm X and Black Muslims." *Detroit News,* March 3, 1965.

McManus, Jane. "The Outlook of Malcolm X." *National Guardian,* April 18, 1964.

Militant, The (By the Editors). "Murder of Malcolm X is a Cruel Blow to the Cause of Black Emancipation." March 1, 1965.

Miller, Loren. "Farewell to Liberals: A Negro View." *The Nation,* October 20, 1962.

Minnis, Jack. A review of *Malcolm X Speaks. Life with Lyndon in the Great Society* (Atlanta), Vol. 1, No. 41, 1965.

Monthly Review (By the Editors). "Aspects of the Birmingham Crisis." June, 1963.

——. "Socialism and the Negro Movement." September, 1963.

——. "The Colonial War at Home." May, 1964.

——. "Decolonization at Home." October, 1965.

Morrison, Allan. "Who Killed Malcolm X?" *Ebony*, October, 1965.

Nadle, Marlene. "Malcolm X: The Complexity of a Man in the Jungle." *Village Voice*, February 25, 1965. (One of the most valuable interviews from the final period.)

National Guardian. "The Black Revolution and the White Backlash." July 4, 1964. (Transcript of the Town Hall forum in New York on ·June 15, 1964, sponsored by the Association of Artists for Freedom. Panelists were Ossie Davis, Ruby Dee, Lorraine Hansberry, LeRoi Jones, John O. Killens, Paule Marshall, Charles E. Silberman and James Wechsler; moderator was David Susskind.)

Neal, Lawrence P. "A Reply to Bayard Rustin – The Internal Revolution." *Liberator*, July, 1965.

——. "Malcolm and the Conscience of Black America." *Liberator*, February, 1966.

Nelson, Truman. "Delinquent's Progress." *The Nation*, November 8, 1965.

New York Herald Tribune (editorial). "Hate: Full Circle." February 23, 1965.

New York Times (editorial). "Malcolm X." February 22, 1965.

Paris, Martin. "Negroes Are Willing to Use Terrorism, Says Malcolm X." *Columbia Daily Spectator*, February 19, 1965. (Report of Malcolm's last formal talk, given at Columbia University on February 18, 1965.)

Parks, Gordon. "'I Was a Zombie Then – Like All Muslims I Was Hypnotized.'" *Life*, March 5, 1965. (Report of Malcolm's last interview, two days before his death.)

Phillips, Waldo B. "Political Implications of Malcolm X's Death." *Los Angeles Herald Dispatch*, March 4, 1965.

Plimpton, George. "Miami Notebook: Cassius Clay and Malcolm X." *Harpers*, June, 1964.

Porter, Herman. Nine articles about the Malcolm X murder trial in New York. *The Militant*, January 24, 31, February 7, 14, 21, 28, March 7, 14, 21, 1966.

Porter, Ruth. "Paris Meeting Hears Malcolm X." *The Militant*, December 7, 1964.

Prattis, P. L. "Malcolm X Trying to Make Racket Out of Desperation." *Michigan Chronicle*, March 28, 1964.

Price, William A. "Malcolm's Death Spotlights Gap Between Negro and White." *National Guardian*, March 6, 1965.

Protz, Roger. "Millions of Britons See Malcolm X in TV Broadcast of Debate at Oxford." *The Militant*, December 14, 1964.

Revolutionary Action Movement (RAM). "Why Malcolm X Died." *Liberator*, April, 1965.

Ring, Harry. "Radio Interview with Malcolm X." *The Militant,* February 8, 1965. (Text of discussion on WBAI-FM, January 28, 1965.)

Robeson, Eslanda. "Malcolm X's Funeral, Dignity and Brotherhood." *Baltimore Afro-American,* March 20, 1965.

Robinson, Jackie. "Bullets Silenced a Man of Courage." *Michigan Chronicle,* March 13, 1965.

Russell, Carlos E. "Exclusive Interview with Brother Malcolm X." *Liberator,* May, 1964.

Rustin, Bayard. "On Malcolm X." *New America,* February 28, 1965.

—— and Kahn, Tom. "The Mark of Oppression." *New America,* March 24, 1965. (Also printed as "The Ambiguous Legacy of Malcolm X," *Dissent,* Spring, 1965.)

——. "Making His Mark." *Book Week,* November 14, 1965.

Samuels, Gertrude. "Feud Within the Black Muslims." *New York Times Magazine,* March 22, 1964.

Shabazz, James. "Weep for Brother Malcolm, He Is Dead." *The Militant,* March 15, 1965. (Memorial address by Malcolm's secretary at Militant Labor Forum in New York.)

Snellings, Rolland. "Malcolm X As International Statesman." *Liberator,* February, 1966.

Spellman, A. B. "Interview with Malcolm X." *Monthly Review,* May, 1964.

——. "The Legacy of Malcolm X." *Liberator,* June, 1965.

Stone, I. F. "The Pilgrimage of Malcolm X." *New York Review of Books,* November 11, 1965.

Strickland, William L. "Epitaph for Malcolm X." *Freedom North* (New York), Vol. I, No. 3, 1965.

Studies on the Left (By the Editors). "Civil Rights and the Northern Ghetto." Summer, 1964.

Sykes, Ossie. See Wilson, C. E.

Thomas, Norman. Letter to *Viewpoint* editorial board. *Viewpoint,* June, 1965. (The Socialist Party leader urges the New York publication of Students for a Democratic Society not to leave the impression that it endorses everything Malcolm stood for.)

Vernon, Robert. "White Radicals and Black Nationalism." *International Socialist Review,* Winter, 1964.

——. "Malcolm X, Voice of the Black Ghetto." *International Socialist Review,* Spring, 1965.

Walker, Wyatt Tee. "Nothing But a Man." *Negro Digest,* August, 1965.

Warde, William F. "The Life and Death of Malcolm X." *International Socialist Review,* Spring, 1965.

Wechsler, James A. "Malcolm X and the Death of Rev. Klunder." *New York Post,* April 13, 1964.

——. "The Cult of Malcolm X." *The Progressive,* June, 1964. (Appraisals by the editor of the *New York Post* after attending Malcolm's talk on "The Black Revolution" on April 8, 1964.)

——. "About Malcolm X." *New York Post,* February 23, 1965.

Weekly People (editorial). "What Killed Malcolm X." March 13, 1965. (The Socialist Labor Party's attitude to Malcolm and black nationalism.)

Williams, Robert F. "The Crusader and Mr. Elijah Muhammad." *The Crusader* (Havana), May, 1963.

——. "Malcolm X: Death Without Silence." *The Crusader,* March, 1965.

Wilkins, Roy. "Malcolm X-ism Jars White Complacency." *Detroit News,* January 3, 1965.

——. "No Time for Avengers." *New York Amsterdam News,* March 6, 1965.

——. "The Repercussions of Malcolm X Death." *Detroit News,* March 7, 1965.

Wilson, C. E. "The Quotable Mr. X." *Liberator,* May, 1965.

—— and Sykes, Ossie. "Malcolm X: A Tragedy of Leadership." *Liberator,* May, 1965.

Woodford, John. "Books Noted." (*The Autobiography of Malcolm X). Negro Digest,* December, 1965.

Worthy, William. "The Angriest Negroes." *Esquire,* February, 1961.

——. "Malcolm X Says Group Will Stress Politics." *National Guardian,* March 21, 1964. (A report of Malcolm's first press conference after the split.)

Young, Whitney, Jr. "Malcolm's Death Solves Nothing." *New York World-Telegram and Sun,* February 25, 1965.

Young Socialist. "Interview with Malcolm X." March-April, 1965. (Indispensable for understanding the evolution of Malcolm's thinking about black nationalism. Also in *Malcolm X Talks to Young People.)*

Unpublished Speech Manuscripts and Transcripts

God's Judgment of White America, December 1, 1963. (Malcolm's last speech as a Black Muslim; in New York.)

Which Way Goes the Negro?, May 23, 1964. (Malcolm's opening remarks in debate with Louis E. Lomax, two days after returning from his first trip to Africa; in Chicago.)

Pierre Berton Show, January 19, 1965. (Malcolm took this occasion to express a number of new and revised positions; in Toronto.)

RELATED LISTENING

Long-Playing Records

Message to the Grass Roots. Afro-American Broadcasting Co., Detroit, 1965. (Excerpts from a speech to the Northern Negro Grass Roots Leadership Conference, Detroit, November 10, 1963. In *Malcolm X Speaks,* Chapter I.)

Malcolm X Speaks Again. Twenty Grand Records, New York, 1965. (Answers to questions, divided into five parts: Violence and Non-Violence; Human Rights and Civil Rights; Birmingham Sunday School Bombing; The Ballot or the Bullet; Black Nationalism. From the transition period – the last week of March or first week of April, 1964.)

Tapes

The Crisis of Racism, May 1, 1962. (A New York symposium sponsored by the Committee to Aid the Monroe Defendants. Speakers were Malcolm X, James Farmer and William Worthy; moderator was Murray Kempton. Malcolm had just returned from Los Angeles, where he had organized the protest against the brutal police attack on the Black Muslims. Question and answer period.)

Talk at City College of New York, November 7, 1963. (A straight Black Muslim speech, although Malcolm forgot to talk about a separate black nation until he was asked about it. Question and answer period.)

The Ballot or the Bullet, April 3, 1964. (A Cleveland symposium sponsored by CORE. The other guest speaker was Louis E. Lomax. In *Malcolm X Speaks,* Chapter III.)

The Black Revolution, April 8, 1964. (A New York talk sponsored by the Militant Labor Forum. In *Two Speeches by Malcolm X* and *Malcolm X Speaks,* Chapter IV. Question and answer period includes exchange with James Wechsler.)

The Ballot or the Bullet, April 12, 1964. (A Detroit talk sponsored by the Group on Advanced Leadership [GOAL]. Content covers much of the material in Cleveland April 3 talk of same name, but not word for word.)

What's Behind the "Hate-Gang" Scare?, May 29, 1964. (A New York symposium sponsored by the Militant Labor Forum. Speakers were Malcolm X, Clifton DeBerry, Quentin Hand and William Reed; moderator was Robert Vernon. Most of text in *Malcolm X Speaks,* Chapter VI. Question and answer period.)

Long John Nebel Show, June 20, 1964. (Panel discussion over New York Station WOR, starting with a discussion of the book *Crisis in Black and White* by Charles E. Silberman. Panelists were Malcolm, Silberman, P.J. Sidney and Martin Berger.)

The Editors Speak, July 4, 1964. (Panel discussion over New York Station WLIB, with Malcolm answering questions about the newly formed OAAU. Panelists were Allan Morrison and George S. Schuyler; moderator was George W. Goodman.

Interview in Cairo, July, 1964. (Malcolm answers questions by Milton Henry about the response to his role at the five-day meeting of the Organization of African Unity. Most of text in *Malcolm X Speaks,* Chapter VII.)

Barry Gray Show, November 28, 1964. (Panel discussion over New York Station WMCA, about the crisis in the Congo. Panelists were Malcolm X, Hugh H. Smythe, Sanford Griffith and James H. Robinson.)

Fragment of talk at OAAU rally, November 29, 1964. (Malcolm's remarks during the last 15 minutes of his first OAAU rally after his second trip to Africa.)

Les Crane Show, December 2, 1964. (Malcolm answers questions in a brief guest appearance over New York station WABC-TV.)

Talk at HARYOU-ACT Forum in Harlem, December 12, 1964. (Question and answer period.)

Talk at OAAU rally, December 13, 1964. (Other speakers were Dick Gregory and Muhammad Babu. In *Malcolm X Speaks,* Chapter VIII.)

Talk at Harvard Law School Forum, December 16, 1964. (Question and answer period.)

Talk at Harlem rally, December 20, 1964. (The rally was called in support of the Mississippi Freedom Democratic Party; one of the speakers was Fannie Lou Hamer. In *Malcolm X Speaks,* Chapter IX.)

Talk at OAAU rally, December 20, 1964. (Malcolm's talk was mainly about Africa. Fannie Lou Hamer also spoke. In *Malcolm X Speaks,* Chapter X.)

Talk to Mississippi youth, December 31, 1964. (Around one-fifth of the text appears in *Malcolm X Talks to Youth* and in *Malcolm X Speaks,* Chapter XI. Question and answer period.)

Prospects for Freedom in 1965, January 7, 1965. (A New York talk sponsored by the Militant Labor Forum. In *Two Speeches by Malcolm X* and in *Malcolm X Speaks,* Chapter XII. Question and answer period; almost whole text in *The Militant,* May 24, 1965.)

Interview with *Young Socialist,* January 18, 1965. (The tape contains about ten minutes not included in the printed version, approved by Malcolm, that appears in *Malcolm X Talks to Young People.)*

Talk at OAAU rally, January 24, 1965. (A talk about Afro-American history. Question and answer period.)

Fragment of talk at London School of Economics, second week of February, 1965.

Talk at Detroit rally, February 14, 1965. (Malcolm's speech under the sponsorship of the Afro-American Broadcasting Co., on the day that his home had been bombed. Most of the text in *Malcolm X Speaks,* Chapter XIII.)

Contact, February 18, 1965. (A phone-in and panel discussion program over New York Station WINS. Panelists were Malcolm X, Aubrey Barnette and Gordon D. Hall; moderator was Stan Bernard. This was Malcolm's last appearance on the air. One-third of the text in *Malcolm X Speaks,* Chapter XIV.)